# CAMP

## INSPIRED BY TRUE STORIES
## FROM ROYAL FAMILY KIDS' CAMP

### WAYNE AND DIANE TESCH

Revised and Updated
Previous edition titled
*From Despair to an Heir: Reviving the Heart of a Child*

While some former campers are now grown and have given us permission to use their names, in most instances throughout this book, campers' names have been changed to protect their identity.

ISBN 0-9898348-0-8

Printed in the United States of America

Royal Family KIDS®
3000 W. MacArthur, Suite 412
Santa Ana, CA 92704
714.438.2494
www.royalfamilykids.org

We dedicate this book to the children
who have overcome the despairs of abuse.
May their hearts be revived with a fresh joy,
their minds renewed with a new purpose,
and their lives rekindled to shine more
brightly than ever before.

# CONTENTS

# ACKNOWLEDGMENTS

**M**any people have influenced the development of Royal Family KIDS, … and of this book.

We thank our parents, who have prayed for us and have done our daily tasks and contributed countless hours to move us along in "growing a dream."

Since our first edition of this book, Diane's mom, Alice Jermy, went to be with the Lord on October 26, 2006. She had been a Camp Grandma for nine years, handing out afternoon snacks to children, among her other tasks at camp. Though she couldn't call her own children by name in the last two years of her life, failing from Alzheimer's disease, she would still haltingly ask, "How are things — over — you know — over — at your — office?" And Diane always knew she meant the Royal Family office. She loved this ministry and was so proud of all that has been done. Diane's dad, Art Jermy, age 89, still collects cans and bottles from the residents on the 18 floors of his retirement tower every night at 8 p.m., walking all 18 stories 'til he reaches the ground floor. He turns, recycles them, and brings the proceeds into Royal Family's office on behalf of our friends at Bethel Towers. Collectively, they now raise over $2,400 a year for "the kids" at Royal Family. The children also thank you!

Wayne's mom, Ruth Tesch, met her Lord on June 5, 2007, after a long illness with diabetes. Mom and Dad Tesch have prayed so much for us during the first 22 years since Royal Family's inception. They too, have supported it with their gifts; and had they have lived closer, would have been more involved in a "hands on" way. Their prayers have been invaluable.

We thank our daughter and son-in-law, Renee and Paul Schroder, and our "Grand Girls," McKenzie and Katie. Thank you, Renee, for praying for us, for seeing our struggles and rejoicing with us at every milestone. Thank you for scheduling the many flights and rental cars to spread the word about RFK across thousands of miles. You make our lives less stressful on the road and in the air! Thank you, Paul, for praying for us and for giving Renee freedom to work "offsite" for us in your home — many times late at night. Your home has been a respite for us while nurturing our dream. McKenzie and Katie, your sweet, cheerful voices and giggles over the phone warm our hearts and lighten our spirits in the pursuit of lifting other children's burdens. We love all of you very much.

We thank Dr. George O. Wood, recently elected to the General Superintendent's Office of the Assemblies of God. We are so proud to have been joined with you for 16 years of ministry, during which you gave us the freedom to try a new idea like Royal Family Kids and moved us beyond P.T.S. (Post Traumatic Syndrome) despair following the first week of Camp by sharing the Starfish Story. Your many sermons are a foundation for this book. Your personal devotionals since that time have spoken clear messages of encouragement and inspiration to Royal Family Camp Directors over the years!

Again, we thank the four angels — you know who you are — for whom Vicki Barnes prayed on that Friday evening in our home. You have lifted us to new heights and helped us soar beyond adversity!

We thank Dr. Dale Berkey and the staff at Berkey Brendel Sheline for mentoring and guiding us in a standard of excellence in ministry and sincere friendship over the many miles.

We thank our office team who work daily to back-up our commitment to the thousands of volunteers on the front lines in the camps. Without our back-up team, the net of camps worldwide would not hold the catch. Keep riding the bus with us!

We thank Julie Fleming who has brought the many resources together to make this book a reality.

We thank Jennie Thomas who assisted with documentation and research to make this edition current.

We thank the Camp Directors, for without your untiring dedication and commitment, the dream of Royal Family KIDS would still be just that — a dream. You have given that dream flesh and bones and have made it breathe life into desperate children.

We thank the many church congregations, some old friends and others, newer, who take on the task and vision of living "true religion" (James 1:27) by caring for the orphans of our day.

Finally, we thank the thousands of Camp Counselors and Staff Members. You are the hands and arms that heal precious children who we come across year after year.

# PART ONE:

A Unique Christian Ministry
to Abused, Abandoned, and
Neglected Children

# INTRODUCTION

This is a dangerous book. Written by crazy persons with radical ideas, their story defies an institution that has been a part of our culture before we were a country. In word and deed, the writers have set out to bring down an enemy so entrenched that any sane person sees the hopelessness of their cause.

And yet, heedless, or perhaps ignorant of the odds against them, they continue their battle. Dear reader, be warned: these rebels are not extraordinary at all, but quite ordinary like you or I. Ordinary, yes, but doing extraordinary things. In humble fashion they will try to convince you to join their cause. As if you have something to offer.

Do not be deceived. In reading this book you might be compelled to make a donation to their cause. As if your money can be used to fight darkness anyway. Did I not mention that they fight an evil? But why let it concern you? This evil is hidden, even though it is passed on generation to generation in a neverending cycle. You and I are excellent at overlooking it, even in our own communities — even our own families.

Please put that light away. We don't want to see this...inconvenience. Why expose this... challenge. It is forgotten. No one wants these children anyway. Their behavior is so... abnormal.

Children. The authors will use the fact that this darkness involves children to tug on your heart. Fine then. Give money to ease your conscience. But please don't encourage this movement by sharing your time.

Please understand. These kids are unlovable. If you give them your time, your compassion and, heaven forbid, love, what can they give you in return? They have nothing to give you for they have nothing. Would you share your love unconditionally with children whose own parents don't even value them? Absurd.

Dear reader, don't let compassion overcome your senses! Do you really want to give up your hard earned vacation time, your golf games, your spa treatments - all to give just a chance for a hopeful future to an abused, neglected and abandoned child?

Let me be plain. If you read on, the authors will force upon you a choice. You cannot go back to your comfortable ignorance. For you see, this book wants you to join a revolution for whom? Well...for what a great revolutionary once called "the least of these."

So please don't cause trouble. Put this book down and pick up the sports section, or perhaps a good romance novel. I can see you are much too wise to join the revolution to reach the hundreds of thousands of children 'in the system' — the foster care system. We both know that the revolution will never succeed anyway... without your help.

Sincerely,
Jacob Roebuck
Writer/Director of the Motion Picture CAMP

# CHAPTER ONE
## *Child Abuse: An Epidemic*

Amy and Amanda showed no emotion. Their innocent faces were pale ... stagnant and subdued ... emotionally withdrawn from everything around them. These young girls had been deprived of sleep — the black bags under their pure eyes were the concrete evidence. Their hair was a disheveled mess. They almost didn't make it to camp.

They missed the early morning registration. It was going to be too late for the girls to be able to come to camp — even though they desperately needed to be there.

But a Camp Director's wife came through for Amy and Amanda and wouldn't take no for an answer! She insisted that these girls be brought immediately to the church. Two special $1,000.00 spots were being held for Amy and Amanda and a Counselor had taken a week of her personal vacation time to volunteer for camp. With some "persistence and encouragement" from the wife of the Camp Director, the girls arrived at the church shortly thereafter.

As Amy and Amanda arrived at camp, their Counselors noticed that they had only one tiny backpack between the two of them. No extra clothes. Even their flip flops were too small for their feet. Neither one had a sleeping bag, a bathing suit or even a pillow.

And yet, that wasn't the most discouraging thing.

Their faces showed no joy ... no laughter ... no curiosity ... no wonder ... no feeling. Whenever anyone would speak to them, they'd look away or shyly ignore them. The traumas of their lives had taken a great toll on them — both inside and out. It was drastically clear — their hearts needed reviving.

However, through the tender, loving care of their Counselor, Donna, a world of difference was made in the lives of Amy and Amanda. By Wednesday, just two days after camp began, Amy and Amanda were clean ... rested ... swimming in their new swimsuits ... running around ... having fun ... jumping up and down ... laughing, talking and smiling — enjoying life just as kids should.

What a change in these two girls! At camp, their hearts were revived, and their lives were changed from that point forward.

It's a national tragedy that this year about 3.6 million reports of children being abused or neglected will be filed, and thousands of other cases of abuse or neglect will go unreported.[1]

Amy and Amanda and children like them live in a horror-filled world, a world in which children dream about monsters that perform horrendous deeds on their bodies but then awaken to the reality that their monsters are *real*. This horror-filled world is full of children who are locked in closets, thrown against walls, pummeled with fists or belts, and told, "I wish you were never born!" They shelter themselves from the outside world by covering physical and emotional wounds; they put on a fake smile, while inside they are dying. They cry hot tears on their pillow at night, and dread the morning light because it could lead to another day of abuse. The dreadful world is crowded with children who tiptoe in their own home or apartment, awaiting the next explosion that launches them once again into the vicious and unending cycle of abuse.

Child abuse is horrific and it is destroying the lives of children all over the world. However, child abuse is not a new problem or a new discovery. In fact, child abuse is not new at all to the abusers or their victims. It is a reality that they must face every day in the privacy of their homes.

We write this book in hopes of enlisting others to help revive the hearts of children. For children paralyzed with fear, this book provides a key to survival, and brings them a ray of hope. For adult Christians, this book provides the key to meaningful action that will allow them to be the arms, legs, and the voice of hope to abused, abandoned, and neglected children.

When a doctor faces a fast-spreading illness, that doctor can choose to try to fight back the illness alone or choose to awaken other medical professionals to help stop the epidemic. That's why we are sounding the alarm to the <u>Christian Church</u>. It is time to stand united and join forces to stop the spread of this horrific epidemic called child abuse in America.

Even if we can't completely *stop* child abuse, we can do our part to *prevent* it, and we can reach out with loving hands to *put back together the lives* of the children who have suffered from abuse, treating them like heirs in a family who loves them. That's why we wanted to write this book.

In the following chapters, you'll learn about the devastating long-term effects that child abuse has on its victims. You'll see the inspirational model God has established for us to follow in responding to this crisis. You'll learn practical steps that the Church can take to mend the broken lives of abused children. Finally, you'll be introduced to Royal Family KIDS, one avenue of healing we, as Christians, have created for abused, abandoned, and neglected children. RFK is a program that we started over 27 years ago that now has served over 78,000 children. Last year, we held 159 camps in 37 states with 24 international camps. We reached over 6,500 children in one year and have a volunteer base of 9,324. Last year, our volunteers, collectively, put in over 1,323,972 hours.

Throughout this book, you'll meet the children and Counselors behind the statistics, children like Joshua, whose whole perspective on his life changed after he learned the words to one of the songs that are sung at camp. His foster mother explained how those words sunk deep into his heart, gave him a new hope, purpose, and a new attitude. The song was titled, *I Am a Promise,* and it was the message of this song that helped revive Joshua's heart back to joy. Here are the words:

*I am a promise, I am a possibility,*
*I am a promise with a capital "P"*
*I am a great big bundle of potentiality.*

*And I am learnin' to hear God's voice*
*And I am tryin' to make the right choices,*
*I'm a promise to be*
*Anything God wants me to be.*

*I can go anywhere that He wants me to go, I*
*can be anything that He wants me to be,*
*I can climb the high mountains, I can cross the wide sea,*
*I'm a great big promise, you see!*

*I am a promise, I am a possibility,*
*I am a promise with a capital "P"*
*I am a great big bundle of potentiality.*

*And I am learnin' to hear God's voice*
*And I am tryin' to make the right choices,*
*I'm a promise to be*
*Anything God wants me to be.*

*I'm a promise to be*
*Anything God wants me to be.*
*(by Gloria Gaither)*

The very next day after returning home from camp, Joshua went to visit his father who was in prison. With sheer excitement and glee, he described all the things he had done at camp and suddenly burst into song — singing every word with his whole heart.

Tears filled the prison that day, as everyone, from other inmates to visiting friends and relatives, and even the guards stood in awe as Joshua sang.

A week later, as Joshua described his camp experience with his mother and the social worker, the same thing happened.

This time, it was his mother and the social worker that were both moved to tears as Joshua belted out the lyrics to the song.

You can probably imagine what happened when Joshua started school the next fall and exclaimed that he had a song to sing for the school talent show!

He remembered every word. That's how important camp had been to him. Children like Joshua need to realize how valuable they truly are. Children like him have little in this world. They don't ask us for very much. They deeply appreciate and love anything we can give them.

Our experiences with the abused, abandoned, and neglected children like this young man have inspired us to write this book, to let Christians see what is being perpetrated on America's children, and to challenge them to do something about it. Christians clothed in God's love are the best hope for abused children, children like Amy, Amanda, and Joshua whom we have met and have learned to love.

After reading this book you will never be the same. You will be moved to tears, challenged to take action, and filled with compassion for the children of this world. You will recognize that every child deserves a chance to be celebrated and not violated.

## CHAPTER TWO
# *The Hard Facts: The Truth Behind Abuse*

God has always loved children, but mankind has not always shared that love. History shows that at different times and in different cultures, children have been used, abused, sacrificed to idols, sold like property, and treated worse than animals. It wasn't until the eighteenth century before the philosopher Rousseau finally awakened the idea that children were humans rather than property when he wrote, "Let us speak less of the duties of children and more of their rights."

What are children's rights? If we could make a Bill of Rights for Children, we would say that children should have the right

- to life
- to be received with joy
- to a gentle upbringing
- to find their unique identity
- to walk with God

These rights won't ever be legislated. They may not even be widely accepted. But on behalf of the children, we must say that they should never learn violence, hatred, fear or ridicule at the hands of their caretakers. This is an ancient, vicious cycle that needs to be broken.

Historically, it has been legal to sell one's children, as was codified as far back as 1792 B.C. by Hammurabi, the ancient Babylonian lawgiver.[1] In 700 B.C., the law called "Patria Protestar" gave a father the right to sell, mutilate, or even kill his offspring.[2] In Old Testament times, it was a man's right to treat his children as property.

In the Bible, when Abraham's nephew Lot took two strangers into his home, the men of his city, Sodom, surrounded the house, demanding that he surrender his two guests. Instead, Lot offered the men his two daughters. "Let me bring them out to you, and you can do what you like with them," Lot says to the mob (Gen. 19:8). Lot's guests were actually angels of God. They rescued Lot and his daughters from the men of Sodom, but Lot was willing to bargain with the very lives of his own children.

The Greek philosopher Aristotle reflected the opinion of his time when he wrote, "The justice of a master or father is different from that of a citizen, for a son or slave is property, and there can be no injustice to one's own property." In ancient Greece, the practice of *pederasty* allowed an adult male to legally court the affections of a boy twelve years old or older. If the arrangement was acceptable to the boy's father, the boy would exchange sexual favors with the suitor in return for training, military equipment, and other gifts. What we would consider to be child abuse today was commonplace in Greek society.[3]

With this in mind, even though child abuse was commonplace, it was never right or considered lightly in the eternal scheme of things. The human sacrifice of babies to the god Molech was despicable in the eyes of Jehovah, the God who rescued little Ishmael from starvation in the wilderness, young Isaac from sacrifice on the altar, and baby Moses from death at the hands of the Egyptians. It was the Lord who called a little child to himself and told his disciples, "Unless you change and become like little children, you will never enter the kingdom of heaven … And whoever welcomes a little child like this in my name welcomes me. But if anyone causes one of these little ones who believe in me to sin, it would be better for him to have a large millstone hung around his neck and to be drowned in the depths of the sea" (Matt. 18:3-6).

In fact, Christ gave special significance to children, saying, "See that you do not look down on one of these little ones. For I tell you that their angels in heaven always see the face of my Father in heaven" (Matt. 18:10).

Like so many of the best ideas of Christianity, the idea that children are cherished by God and ought to be cherished by adults has not blossomed easily.

During the Industrial Revolution, children legally worked in coal mines, lumber mills, factories — places that we would not even think of sending a child. These children were sentenced to work long, grueling days. It was during the Industrial Revolution that child abuse was finally recognized, all because of a young girl named Mary Ellen.

### Mary Ellen: The First Case Study

In 1874, Mary Ellen lived with her adoptive parents, but it wasn't much of a life. She was chained to her bed, fed only bread and water, and was often ill. A church worker who was visiting an elderly woman in Mary Ellen's tenement learned of the young girl's plight and decided to do something to help her.

When church workers and Nurse Etta Wheeler came to Mary Ellen's home, they found her badly beaten body still chained to the bedpost. She was barely alive. But local authorities told the church workers they could do nothing because no law on the books prevented a parent from treating a child any way the parent pleased. Out of desperation, the church turned to Henry Bergh, the founding spirit behind the American Society for the Prevention of Cruelty to Animals. Would *he* help Mary Ellen? After all, she was a part of the "animal kingdom."

The ASPCA came to the rescue and removed the young girl as if she were an abused animal. They brought the parents to court for the crime of abuse. Mary Ellen was carried into court on a stretcher, her emaciated and battered body showing the evidence of vicious treatment. Mary Ellen was removed from the parents' custody, and they were given a term in a penitentiary.[4]

People of that day were shocked to realize that the question of cruelty of animals had been regarded as more important than the question of cruelty to children. As a result, the battle for child protection was first taken on by a society for the protection of animals — because that is how children had been regarded by the culture.

It is interesting to note that it was the church workers who discovered Mary Ellen's plight and fought for her well-being. Down through history, the Christian Church has tried to cope with the business of child protection. In the 1600s, the Church established the "poor laws," one of which stated that if a family could not economically provide for their children, the church overseers had the right to remove those children from the home and place them in better circumstances.

This, then, is the historical perspective of child abuse:

- It is an age-old problem.
- It had not been recognized as abuse until the nineteenth century and the case of Mary Ellen.
- Eventually America incorporated laws to protect abused, abandoned, and neglected children, who were most often removed from their homes and placed in civil institutions rather than with volunteer agencies.
- Certain people and the Church have always tried to do away with child abuse and act as a light in this dark part of society.
- In 1960, through the book "Battered Child's Syndrome," Americans finally recognized the need to do something significant, almost 100 years after the Mary Ellen case.

Yet in spite of the laws, every six hours a child dies from abuse or neglect in our society.[5]

**Today**

This shocking statistic shows us that child abuse is not only history, but that it is still very prevalent in today's society. According to the U.S. Department of Health and Human Services Administration for Children and Families:

- This year approximately 3.6 million cases of child abuse or neglect are expected to be reported.[6]
- These cases involve the maltreatment of approximately six million children.[7]
- Children seven and under account for 54 percent of all reported child abuse cases —50.7 percent are girls, 47.3 percent are boys.[8]
- One in five children are solicited sexually while on the internet.[9]
- Nearly 70 percent of all reported sexual assaults occur to children 17 and under.[10]
- Between 75 and 90 percent of reported physical abuse and neglect cases involve the caretakers of the abused children. Another 6.8 percent were other relatives.[11]

Sources also show that the correlation between abuse as a child and the potential for juvenile or adult criminal behavior is appalling:

- In one study, every death-row inmate in San Quentin reported growing up in a violent, abusive environment.[12]
- 97 percent of hard-core juvenile delinquents report a history of severe physical punishment and even assault in their home.[13]
- "There is a strong correlation between girls entering prostitution and various forms of child abuse — including sexual, physical, and emotional. A high percentage of girl prostitutes have been victims of incest, rape, beatings, neglect, and other domestic violence and related problems. The Huckleberry House Project reported that 90% of the girl prostitutes had been sexually molested."[14]

Although these statistics are daunting, do they mean that

child abuse is worse today than it was in the past? We don't really think so. It's just that society is only beginning to understand and take a public stand in the world in which these victims live.

The fact that the frequency and severity of child abuse has still remained a scourge in our society is incredible, because when we have been willing to listen, people everywhere have had a story of abuse to tell. We have heard stories from individuals at the shopping center, the barbershop, the bank, and even in the church.

- In Sacramento, California, we were shopping when a saleswoman asked if we were visiting the area. When we told her we were in town to tape a television news interview about the Royal Family ministry, the woman began to share her story. "I was raised by my father. My mother abused my brother and me, but the courts wouldn't believe my father and refused to move us into his custody. Finally my grandmother gave him Polaroid pictures that showed wounds all across my back from a beating my mom had given me with an electric cord when I was four. I don't remember most of what my mom did to me, but I do remember her making my brother stand in the corner of the room while she knocked his head into the corner to discipline him. She did this a lot."

- Waiting at the barbershop, a friend of the barber sat and had coffee and donuts with us. "I think what you're doing is really needed," he began, and we could tell a story was on the way. "My dad beat us. As we got older, his abuse got worse. I think he was hardest on me because I am the oldest. I remember one day when I was a freshman in high school, he beat me so hard that he knocked my top teeth backward, broke my jaw, and gave me a black eye."

- When we went to open a bank account, the new-account representative, a woman named Carla, asked if we could help her son. Her story was heart-rending. Carla's husband had been a violent alcoholic who abused both her and their children. Before he had committed suicide, he had cold-bloodedly murdered their nine-year-old son, then shot and wounded the seven-year-old and three-year-old boys. It was the youngest one, Carey, whom she hoped we could help. Since his father's death, Carey had turned morose and melancholy. He suffered horrible nightmares. He still wet the bed.

- In Illinois, at a mission conference, we shared some information about the problems of child abuse. Following the service, a young woman sought us out and said, "I'm glad you talked about child abuse tonight. You shared a statistic — that 90 percent of the prostitutes walking the streets of America today were sexually victimized as young girls. You're from Southern California. I used to 'work the streets' between First and Fourth Streets on Harbor Boulevard in Santa Ana. Somehow God came into my life and saved me from all of that. Now I live here, I have a husband and two children who love me. But I really could have used a camp like yours when I was a child."

- In Minneapolis, Minnesota, after a chapel service at North Central Bible College, a young woman approached us with tears running down her face. She said, "Thank you for sharing about child abuse this morning. I was one of those young girls you talked about. But I want you to know these tears are not tears of sorrow. These are tears of joy that *finally* someone is talking about child abuse the way it is."

It's shocking that so many total strangers share their stories of child abuse with us just because we are willing to listen. Many times, all people need is someone to listen and care. It is time for us to listen for the cries of those who are lost in this tragic world of abuse. With this book, we are sounding a call and, at the same time, portraying how to revive the hearts of the children.

Statistics show that about one in four adult women and one

in six adult men were abused as children.[15] Hypothetically, of your four best female friends, one was probably an abused child. Of the six male members of your Bible study, one was probably an abused child. In fact, you may have been abused as a child, yourself.

If this is the case, this isn't a book to tell you how to deal with those memories. But if you are still haunted by that abusive past, let us quickly share something that you absolutely must believe: **What happened to you wasn't your fault, and you must not blame yourself.** Child abuse (including sexual abuse) is perpetrated by sick adults, and you were in no way responsible. When you were a child, you had no control over the situation. You could have done nothing to prevent it. Don't blame yourself. That is a mistake. If you are still troubled by what happened to you, talk to your pastor or a Christian counselor. There is hope for you. Your past doesn't have to haunt you. It's over, and you can live a victorious life from this day forward.

# CHAPTER THREE

## *A Lifetime of Scars: The Long-Term Effects of Child Abuse*

Abuse is perpetual; once it has been inflicted on someone, it can affect the emotions of that person for life. Individuals who suffered abuse as children may forever deal with the emotional and physical scars it leaves. These scars can cripple their relationships, self-esteem, and their future if they do not get help. One act of abuse can leave a scar in the mind and heart of a person for a lifetime.

That is why it is very important we reach children at an early age (7-11) so they will not have to deal with this horrible problem for years to come. If we can reach them early and teach them through love, then we can start working on the scars that have been inflicted upon their bodies, minds, and emotions. Although some individuals live with these scars their entire lives, one encounter with God's love can heal the bruises of their past, revive their heart, and renew their mind for as long as they live.

In order to help heal these scars, we must know what we are facing. In every child who has faced abuse, abandonment, or neglect, there are three monumental scars:

### Scar #1: Death of Trust

Because so often child abuse and neglect involve the child's caregiver, trust is one of the major casualties in the battle. The first person children trust in their lives is the hand that rocks the cradle. What then becomes of trust if that hand also breaks, bruises, and maims?

The person that they should be able to rely on for love and protection turns out to actually be the enemy. They cannot rely on their caregivers to protect them, so they must learn to protect themselves. This mistrust of the primary adults in their lives is often transferred to all adults. If their parents, grandparents, and stepparents aren't to be trusted, then no one is.

This distrust is demonstrated at lights-out time at our camps. At *any* kids' camp, lights-out time is rowdy enough, with dorms full of children not wanting to settle down and end a day of fun one moment before they absolutely have to. But at a camp for abused, abandoned, and neglected children, this problem is intensified even more. For many of our young campers, abuse at home begins when the lights go out. Sexual abuse in particular may be strongly associated with the dark and silence. The children are reluctant to sleep because they fear an abuser might try to hurt them. Dreams and nightmares also haunt many of the children.

For these reasons, we start our lights-out procedures early in the evening to give the campers lots of time to settle in and get to sleep. The very first year of camp, as I made rounds to help the Counselors get the boys to bed, I noticed that Alan was sleeping with his head on the Bible he had received earlier that day. When I saw Alan the next morning, I asked him why he was using his Bible as a pillow. "Oh," he said, "it makes me feel safe to sleep with my head on the Bible."

For Alan, sleeping on the Scriptures made him feel safe, but many abused children never feel safe again, by day or by night. Some young children sleep with layers of clothes on to make molestation more difficult. For some children, even the casual touch of an adult is a cause for hysteria. Many of the children have an impaired capacity for intimacy. Their innocence and childhood have been murdered.

## Scar #2: Perpetual Anger

Children in our society are taught to honor adults. Because of the size difference between children and adults, children often realize that they can't defend themselves against an adult attacker. It is impossible for children to vindicate themselves on an adult who is abusing them. The result is a perpetual anger that has no avenue for expression. As adults, we know that pent-up anger must be released, or it will work itself out in ways that are generally not related to the subject of the anger. Abused children handle their anger in the same way.

Whereas an adult stands a fighting chance of escaping abuse or overcoming abusers, children have no such hope. The situation of an abused child is analogous to that of a mouse in a trap: The mouse is in constant pain, but it cannot escape. Terrifying rage can result.

Take Erick for example. When Erick first attended our original camp, he came to be known at camp as "Erick the Biter." He was a hyperactive, ADHD child, and had been born already addicted to heroin as an infant. At times, he lashed out at Camp Counselors or the other children like an angry dog — by biting his victim in the rear end.

Most of the day, Erick was like a little water bug, darting from here to there. He was physically delayed in stature for an eight-year-old and very hyper. He had a temper with a very short fuse! If he was provoked by an adult or a child, he would fly off the handle and begin to fight. He could not hold his anger inside, and lashed out at every opportunity. It seemed he couldn't control it at all.

He was afraid for anyone to touch him in fear that they would harm him. One night his Camp Counselor, Leland, stood talking to Erick as he was putting him to bed on the top bunk. Apparently Leland had encroached upon Erick's personal space a little too much. Erick hit him right in the face — for seemingly no reason at all. This was Erick's customary way of releasing his anger. Leland was only there to make sure he was ready for bed, and Erick thought he was there for other reasons. Leland didn't recoil, like most of us would want to. He just continued to show him love and respect throughout the week and assured him he was only there to help him.

The following year, Erick returned to camp — a challenging child behaviorally, but now, he seemed to get so much more out of the chapel times, recreation and socialization. He was still strongly medicated but demonstrated behavior issues in spite of it. He was never comfortable with the Counselors but instead saw them as enemies. In what was to be his third year of camp he didn't show up, and we learned it was because he was in a treatment unit of the hospital due to behavioral issues. He was having a hard time coming to grips with his emotional and trust issues.

Children who have been abused *ought* to be angry about it. This anger, which cannot be directed toward the adult abuser, is then funneled wherever it can go. Peer relationships can be devastated, for abused children cannot relate to other children without their powerful anger interfering. Many abused children act out at school and on the playground, letting their misplaced aggressions destroy their friendships.

If the abuse is not addressed, the anger becomes bitterness. For abused children, bitterness becomes a way of life. It is not really shocking that the only way out of the bitterness and anger for some children is suicide. For others, this rage can turn outward. Statistics over time have proven many convicted murderers were the victims of child abuse.[1]

Because abused children are forced to deny their true feelings, especially feelings of anger, they are often incapable of identifying their true feelings themselves.[2]

At the RFK Camp in Poulsbo, Washington, an eight-year-old girl demonstrated this kind of anger by "shredding" a bench built of two-by-fours. After an RFK staff member reported the damage to the camp manager and offered to pay for the damage, the camp manager said it was not necessary to replace the bench. The manager's only concern was how the young girl was doing.

## Scar #3: Self-Hatred and Self-Mutilation

The developmental years of children's lives determine their self-image. Young children tend to regard any pain or unpleasantness in their lives as their own fault. Many, many abused children believe the abuse happens because they are in some way bad or have done something bad — particularly because much abuse happens in the name of punishment for misdeeds. Sometimes, children can also develop self-destructive habits where they are hurting themselves, to deal with the pain of abuse, as well. That's exactly what Matthew dealt with ...

Matthew was a cute, round-faced seven-year-old boy with a kind and gentle demeanor. However on the inside was a nervousness that made him constantly pick at his fingers until they bled. No matter how he tried, he could not resist the urge to pick. When he first arrived at Royal Family KIDS Camp, all 10 fingers were covered with scotch tape concealing the self-inflicted wounds from his incessant picking. Scotch tape offered no real protection, as his wounds were infected and constantly bleeding. Every moment his hands were idle, he began to pick at his fingers. When Dave, his Counselor, asked the reason why, Matthew's reply was, "I like it!"

Matthew didn't know what caused this action ... he just knew it was something he desired to do. Dave knew that in order to work on this problem he must first help bandage Matthew's current wounds. Dave washed Matthew's hands, cleaned him up, and put on band-aids. After all, if Matthew could not see his fingers, then there would not be the urge to pick at them. For the moment, he was protected from himself.

It didn't take long until the band-aids fell prey to deterioration from camp activities such as swimming, building, painting, and brushing his teeth. Band-aid upon band-aid was not effective. Once these band-aids were gone, Matthew was back to his old ways. Kids started asking him a lot of questions about his wounds. This questioning from the other kids only made matters worse.

After hearing the talk from the other children, Dave set a goal that by weeks' end, Matthew would not wear band-aids or have any wounds. Whatever it took, he was going to see Matthew freed from his desire to pick his fingers. It was going to be a tough road, but he was determined to see progress over the week at camp.

One night during music time, Matthew and Dave were sitting together on a bench. Matthew looked down and saw an imperfection on Dave's hand and began to pick at it. Matthew looked up at him as if to say, "Can't you see this needs attention?" He continued to pick at Dave's hand with reckless abandon. Dave was going to stop him but soon realized the plan to distract Matthew from picking at his own hands was actually working ... even if it meant his own hand was being picked at in the process. He had vowed to save Matthew's fingers at any cost, so he endured and let him pick at his hand.

All of the sudden, Dave felt a burning sensation on his left hand and began to react because of the pain. He looked down and saw blood. Matthew grabbed his hand quick and was proud to show him the wound. Matthew looked up at him with warm eyes and said, "This needs a band-aid." Dave asked, "Will you help me put it on?"

By sacrificing a little of himself, Dave made a difference in Matthew's life. From that night on Matthew didn't pick at his hands again. Dave had put his own comfort on the line to help save a child's heart.

When Matthew boarded the bus to leave camp, he wore no

band-aids and had no wounds. He had been freed from the terrible habit of picking at his fingers, at least for a week. All it took was one person willing to pay the price.

When the bus pulled out from camp on the last day, Dave stood outside the bus to wave goodbye, and when he looked down, saw one compassionately placed band-aid. He smiled as he remembered the sacrifice and cherished the band-aid covering a wound that he had bore for Matthew.

Too many abused children never make the discovery that Matthew made. For them, their self-image has died painfully.

If abused children believe that abuse is their fault because they are bad, they often abandon themselves to this "badness" and let it become a self-fulfilling prophecy. Abused children express their self-hatred through self-destructive behavior. Some of them subconsciously set themselves up for abuse, thinking they somehow deserve it because they are "bad."

Abused children internalize their feelings of helplessness and isolation only to find that these feelings haunt them throughout their lives. Because many abused children are forced to go to great lengths to try to hide what is happening to them, they may be forced to withdraw from normal peer relationships at an early age. They may find themselves isolated and cut off from those they see as normal.

This isolation can result in many sad, lost years, and it may manifest itself differently in boys and girls, mainly because of the prevailing attitudes about male and female roles in our society. Even today in America, girls are raised to be more caring and gentle, "weaker" if you will, than boys. Young girls who are abused may turn into "permanent victims." Boys in our society, on the other hand, are socialized to be more aggressive and physical than girls are. A boy who has been abused may respond with hostility and aggression.[3] Furthermore, the abused boy may become the one who victimizes others. This is evident in the high number of male convicts who were abused as children: Two of every three prisoners convicted of first-degree murder report childhood histories of physical abuse.[4]

## Scars Can Be Healed

Although the scars of child abuse are varied and complex, they can be healed. The Church can and ought to be part of the healing process. The Church can become the arms of the Lord taking care of neglected children as the psalmist expresses: "Though my father and mother forsake me, the Lord will receive me" (Ps. 27:10).

Through His body, the Church, the Lord has taken care of people. People like Marie. I met Marie at a 10th Year Camp Anniversary Celebration for the Topeka, KS camp in 2005. As I mingled with guests, this young woman approached me and introduced herself. She said, "You don't know who I am, but I attended one of your camps in Orange County, California, for three years as a child." I was excited, because this was one of the first grown up campers we had encountered face to face up to that point — and she was 2,000 miles from where she had attended camp for three years.

Marie told me her story of how she was raised by loving, Christian foster parents. They had sent her to camp in California, and it had changed her life forever. She was once devastated by abuse and neglect, but she had received a new life at RFK. She went on to introduce me to her husband and told me, "We're happily married, we have three beautiful children and I don't beat my kids. Because the cycle of abuse has been broken."

As I returned to the office, we began making plans for Marie and her husband to attend our March Celebration Banquet so we could introduce her to the audience and interview her. Because they lived so close, her foster parents were invited to attend also and share in this moment of Marie being reconnected with Royal Family KIDS. At the end of her interview on stage, she presented a dozen red roses to her foster mom and dad in gratitude for all they had done for her — and for sending her to RFK. What a thrill to see the long-term effects of a life transformed by the childhood experience she had been given at Royal Family KIDS.

To finish telling you about Erick the Biter, his story did not end with his stay in the hospital. The following year, he returned for his final year of camp. He was now 12 and would "graduate" from RFK. At Friday's graduation ceremony, Erick, who had matured considerably from his first year with us, stood before an audience of about 60 campers and implored his fellow campers, "It's going to be sad not to be able to come back here and see you guys next year. But I want you to know, you can make it. I was pretty messed up myself, and God has made a difference in my life. And He will make a difference in your life." Through God's love, Erick was able to be changed and deal with his emotional issues. No longer was he bound by despair, but he had a new outlook because of RFK.

We didn't see Erick again for seven more years. In 1998, we attended a wedding at Newport-Mesa Christian Center, in Costa Mesa, California (where we were on staff when RFK was birthed 13 years earlier.) While at the wedding, my former Executive Assistant, Bobbi Estrada, approached us with an envelope with a letter from Erick enclosed. It had been seven years since that memorable moment with Erick in the camp graduation ceremony. Diane could hardly open the envelope fast enough as we drove away from the church en route to home. Our eyes filled with tears as she began to read Erick's letter.

3-19-98

Dear Pastor Wayne Tesch,
Hey how are you? I'm doing ok, I'm just trying to walk with the Lord the best I can. I just want to say thanks for everything you've done for me. You've been a real blessing to me, and

my family.

Well it's been 7 years since I've seen you, and God's put it on my heart to ask you this. Do you remember on the last day of Royal Family KIDS Camp, you sat me down and said to me that I can always come back if I wanted to? Well, ever since I left I've been thinking about what you said. So I guess what I'm trying to say is can I come back, and be a part of your ministry?

You guys have touched many people. You have taught these kids that no matter what they go through there is someone that loves them, and that's Jesus Christ. You have also taught these kids that they can accomplish anything with Jesus Christ. (Luke 1:37) For nothing is impossible with God.

Well, just like you were a part of my life, I want to be a part of theirs. I want to work with them, and show them God's love. So I guess you're wondering what's up with me. Well, I just graduated from High School, and I have a job making seven dollars an hour. I also got my license this month. I thank God every day for everything he's done for me. I want to be in Ministry, and work with kids. Eventually I'm going to trade school to become an electrician. (I turn 19 this July 2nd.)

Well, I guess I better go. I have to work tomorrow morning. Please write back and let me know what God's done in your lives. God Bless you all. It was an honor talking to you.

>Love Always.
>Your Brother in Christ,
>Erick

P.S.     All things work for good for those who love the Lord.
What's up Fire Marshall John, Mr. Ed, Grandpa & Grandma McNutt and Pastor Wayne?

Heading for the Royal Family KIDS Camps,
Heading for a lot of fun.
It's great just knowing I'm a part of God's family
Playing under the sun.
Splashing and splashing and having a good time.
Grandpa and Grandma reading a devotion.
It's the great time for the good news that God loves me.

We were overjoyed and speechless. Though we had received reports from caregivers of how much the week means to these children, even we would sometimes question how much they would remember. We're human too! His letter clearly showed that he did remember. In fact, camp had been a turning point for him.

The next week we placed a call to Erick and invited him to

come up to our office in Costa Mesa. The day came and he walked into our office — big, tall, stocky and a grown young man, wearing a baseball cap and Levis. With him came his friend whom he introduced. Then his friend left. "Erick," I inquired, "did you drive yourself up here?"

"Oh no. I couldn't get the car to use. I paid my friend to drive me here."

"Erick, how much did he charge you to drive you here?" I asked.

"I paid him $20."

Feeling bad that this young man had to pay $20 for a 30-minute drive, I said, "Erick, I am so sorry you paid that much to come here."

And before I could pull out a $20 bill to give him, Erick said, "Oh, Pastor Tesch, I would have paid a million dollars to see you again."

I took Erick out to dinner and gave him his choice of anything on the menu at Kaplan's Delicatessen. He said, "I never get a steak in a restaurant. Could I order a steak?"

"Erick, you order anything you want on the menu," I replied. So he did.

Diane remembers the story following my dinner with Erick ...

*Wayne called me and asked me to come pick Erick up and drive him home. Erick and I swapped stories about camp on the drive home, and then he invited me in to meet his mom (legal guardian), who had brought him to camp those three years.*

*When I asked Erick if he had kept any of his things from camp, he shrugged and said, "Yeah."*

*"Erick," his mom said, "go to your room and get your box. Go on. Go on!"*

*Finally with a little coercing, he went down the hall and came back carrying a cardboard file box, the kind with the hand holes in each end. He set it on the floor in front of me and took off the lid. I couldn't believe what was before me — a box nearly full of his*

*Camp memories. He had six T-shirts — two for each year he attended camp, plus one that we had all autographed and sent to him in the treatment center. (During the summer he missed camp, the staff heard about him being in the hospital so they passed around a camper T-shirt for everyone to sign and sent it to his family to deliver to him in the hospital.) It was in tatters — the marker pens were nearly faded beyond recognition, all the colors washed out, neck, sleeves and hem ragged from hundreds of trips through the washing machine. His mom said, "From the time he received that shirt, he wore it EVERY night for at least a year, unless it was in the wash."*

*He had taken all his camp photos from each year and removed them from the original Memory Books and put them all in chronological order in one album. He had every Camper Activity Book he had received during those three years. What a treasure box! And he was so proud of it.*

He was trying his best to be a Christian, and we were so encouraged that a young man who once was bitter and angry was now on the right track. It is amazing to see what love can conquer and what trust can overcome.

For others, their story unfortunately won't be nearly as cheerful. They will stay locked in the horrors of abuse, dealing with the memories of the past with no hope for their future. We must not sit by and let our children become another statistic! We must call ourselves to action! And although we cannot make a difference for all the millions of children who will be abused this year, we can, as the Church, strive to make a difference for as many as we possibly can.

# CHAPTER FOUR

## *The Beginning:*
## *The Dream and the Means*
## *for Change*

In our farewell service from Newport-Mesa Christian Center in 1990, Diane and I recounted the steps God had led us through to arrive at the threshold of beginning Royal Family KIDS. We talked about the day I came home in July 1990 and told Diane I had decided to resign and develop a full-time ministry for abused children. Diane had thought, *It's either another one of Wayne's "great ideas," or he's going into a midlife crisis.*

Diane was used to my great ideas. Through 40 years of marriage, every week — Diane says sometimes it's every *day* — I have come home excited, saying, "You'll never believe this great idea! I know we can do this!"

Diane often tells me, "Wayne, if you accomplish even one or two of your great ideas in this lifetime, you'll be a success." But this time she suspected I was serious. For 18 years I had been the associate pastor of Newport-Mesa Christian Center, a healthy, thriving church in Southern California. Resigning from the church was a big step.

God had already assured Diane that Royal Family KIDS Camps should become an independent ministry early that summer. It was the last day of camp, Friday afternoon June 29, 1990 — the day the children return to their homes. But that year, something a bit different was planned.

All the foster moms and dads and the caretakers of the children had been invited to come early to pick them up so the children could put on a program for them. During the course of the week, the children had been learning songs for a program. For these children, most of whom have short attention spans, it was a major undertaking to learn five songs. But they did it!

We walked into Newport-Mesa Christian Center, where the foster families and caregivers had gathered to pick up their children. The entire choir loft was filled with nearly 100 young children, each wearing a new white Royal Family KIDS Camp T-shirt and a golden Burger King crown to carry out the Royal Family theme. Diane remembers that God seemed to be speaking to her that day: "Look at this. This is a glimpse of what eternity will be like if you just keep bringing children to me one at a time."

It's obvious that God brought about His will in our lives through very special circumstances, but this chapter explains that if God has given you a dream — a great idea — He will give you the means to make it come true.

This is our experience, but we encourage you to recognize that God uses many different approaches based on our own personalities and our backgrounds. God uses His Word in places of solitude so that we can hear His voice. God uses circumstances, conflict, role models, and speakers' illustrations. He uses times of worship and supernatural revelations. He places within our souls the direction and desire to follow our Lord and Savior, Jesus Christ. In addition to all this, He places alongside of us significant adults — men and women — to make sure that the gifts and skills developed in us will bring honor and glory to Him.

This chapter outlines six steps that God used to bring the RFK ministry to abused, abandoned, and neglected children. Those of you who are familiar with Dr. Robert Schuller's sermon,

"Ten Building Blocks of a Dream" will see his influence in these thoughts.

While I was at Newport-Mesa Christian Center, I founded Sonshine Day Camp, a 10-week day camp designed for working parents with children between the ages of six and 12. I also began Sonshine KIDS Camp, a one-week residence camp for children ages nine to 12. The camp was held up in the mountains, the "great cathedral of the outdoors." Next was a 10-week day camp called Young Teen Summer Adventure and a program called Summer Splash for both junior high and high school students.

From these camps, Royal Family KIDS emerged and grew from 37 children the first year, with only our church participating in 1985, to more than 155 camps across the country in 2012.

Why all this emphasis on camping? Children find God at Christian camps. That's where I found God, and it was there that God gave me direction in my life. We wanted to duplicate that model for hundreds of thousands of children.

When we arrived at Newport-Mesa Christian Center in 1972, I was given the freedom to develop camps. At the time, I had no idea of working with abused, abandoned, and neglected children. But God had the great idea. God was putting Diane and me through the laboratory of life so we could develop the skills and gifts necessary to bring Royal Family KIDS into existence.

That's the first step in how dreams come true: *Dreams that catch our imagination and inspire our wills always begin in the mind of God.* We hadn't planned to launch a camp for abused, abandoned, and neglected children one day in the mid-1980s, but God had that plan. The dream begins in the mind of God and is imparted to the heart of the dreamer.

The second step is this: *God connects the dream to the dreamer.* Imagine God walking the balcony of heaven, peering over the rail, looking across the earth, looking for men, women, teenagers, boys, and girls to whom He can entrust His dream. He says,

"There's one." Then out of His compassion and mind and heart, He plants a seed into a dreamer's mind and heart. He plants it in a man or woman or boy or girl whom He will prepare for the job He has planned for them. Look at Noah, Joseph, Moses, Nehemiah, David, Deborah, and Paul. These people are all examples of men and women who were brought to the kingdom with a specific task at a specific time.

Thousands of people accomplish God's will without ever preaching a sermon on Sunday morning. Instead, they preach illustrated life messages every day of the week. They let their pulpit be their executive desk or their workbench in the shop. It happens at a teacher's desk in a classroom or a nurse's station at the hospital. Their congregations are their family, their friends, their associates, or their students. They are ordinary people touched by the dreams that God has placed within their hearts.

Where did God connect the dream to me? When I was 12, the Lord gave me a vision. I believe that vision was God's way of planting His dream in my life. He showed me that vision at three distinct times in my life. The first time, I was twelve years old, attending a kids' camp called Lakeview Gospel Camp, near Lake Ontario in upstate New York. It was a Thursday night, a night I will always remember. I was in the Quonset-shaped tabernacle with wooden benches and sawdust for a floor. Kneeling there by myself, I prayed, "Dear God, I'm 12 years old. What am I supposed to do?" A picture came to my mind, a picture of hundreds of thousands of kids, a sea full of faces that were African-American, Caucasian, Hispanic, and Asian.

When my mom picked me up on Saturday, she asked what happened at camp. I announced, "Mom, God has called me to be a youth pastor and work with kids. I'm moving to California because I'm going to be a preacher."

I still chuckle at my mom's response: "Dear God. Not another preacher in the family." She knew all too well the financial hardship of ministers in fledgling churches.

The second time I saw the vision, I was 24 years old. Diane and I had just moved from New York, and I had set up my office at Newport-Mesa Christian Center. The office was a classroom with an eight-foot folding table and a folding chair. I was sitting in my chair in the new office, looking at the back wall, and again I prayed, "Here I am at a new position, Lord. What do you want me to do?" It was as if God put a slide in a projector and flashed up on the wall the picture I had seen when I was 12 years old, with hundreds of faces projected on the bare wall — African-American, Caucasian, Hispanic, Asian. I decided that I had better get started, and I set out to form ministries for our church's children.

The third time God connected the dream to me was in 1985, when I was 36 years old. I was in the chapel at the campground where we held the very first RFK camp. As I looked over the pews on Thursday evening, I saw a microcosm of the dream that God had given me 24 years earlier. But this time what I saw was not a dream; it was reality. There were African-American, Caucasian, Hispanic, and Asian children staring up at me. All of a sudden the dream was living and breathing. I knew that it was more than just my dream; it was God who had prepared that time and that place. God connected the dream with the dreamer.

The third step in the fulfillment of the dream is this: *The dream alters your schedule.* The dream enters a gestation period. God has given the dream a life of its own, and it becomes all-consuming. That's the way it is with the dream that God imparts from His heart to your heart. You begin to study. You begin to pray. You begin to find information. You write. You read. You become involved in developing strategies to accomplish the dream. You act on plans to make the dream a reality. You reach out, and you begin to feel the pain within your heart. You begin to sense the hurt of the people you're helping. You go through an incredible experience in order to see the dream fulfilled. For us, this had begun to occur since the inception of Royal Family KIDS in 1985.

I was doing more to develop the dream because it continued to demand more and more of my time. The gestation period strains the patience of the dreamer waiting for the birth of the dream. I began to ask God, "Why can't it happen right now? Why is it taking so long? Will I ever live to see the dream fulfilled?"

While the dreamer waits, the rhythm beats, *Plod on. Keep going. Press on. Plod on. Don't quit.* It is patience that identifies those who fulfill the divine dream. Impatient dreamers look for shortcuts and cheap discounts at the price of being faithful. Impatient dreamers will discover that in choosing the painless, easy road, they are in fact walking down the path of shame, boredom, and failure. The dreamer must realize that it takes time — sometimes years — to develop the dream God has imparted.

Christ knew at the age of 12 that He had a mission to accomplish in His lifetime. At age 30 He finally began the mission. David was crowned king when he was 30 years old. David never built the temple he dreamed of building, but his son Solomon accomplished what David desired.

Your dream may take time to develop. Be patient, for God is working out the plans for you. "'For I know the plans I have for you,' declares the Lord, 'plans to prosper you and not to harm you, plans to give you hope and a future'" (Jer. 29:11).

While you wait, plan, and plod on, enjoy the wonderment of asking, *What will happen?* Remember that all the while, God is already at work on the next step. "Being confident of this, that he who began a good work in you will carry it on to completion until the day of Christ Jesus" as we are told by Paul in Philippians 1:6.

Step four in watching the dream come true is this: *Support comes from unexpected sources.*

The RFK Camp in Iowa found that out. They had so many volunteers drop out one year, they thought they would have to cancel the camp. But, for every person who dropped out, God brought somebody to fill the empty spot. They are still going strong today. Why? Because from places you never think, He sends the dreamer the means to carry out the dream.

At our camp in Georgia, so many miracles like this have taken place! Every year they must overcome obstacles. The biggest obstacle was in the Camp Director's third year of camp. She took the initiative to change churches for the camp that year. In addition, they were having a hard time raising the money and finding a way to transport everything to camp. They overcame this challenge by finding out a man at church who built cabinets had a very large trailer. They asked him if they could use the trailer to transport their stuff. He said yes, on one condition — that they would let him haul it down and back with his truck! What a miracle. He brought the trailer to the Camp Director's house about a week prior and every time she saw that trailer sitting in the driveway, she knew God was telling her that He would provide for EVERY camp need — including finances.

When camp came, they still did not have the money. She took her checkbook to Royal Family knowing she would have to help pay for the campground. So, she wrote a check personally to pay for the camp. But when she got home from camp, there was a check from a grant that she didn't think they were going to get, waiting in her mailbox. The amount was exactly the amount to pay her back and pay for the rest of the Royal Family merchandise! Since then, finances have come more easily, and God has always provided!

Following the third year of camp in Southern California, we became frustrated that we weren't doing more to impact abused children in our county. After we shared this frustration with the Camp Grandma, Marita McNutt, she asked us a most obvious question: "Why don't you involve additional churches to duplicate what you are already doing?"

Although this was the obvious way to impact more children's lives, when Diane heard the word *duplicate*, her mind went back to her earlier days of working in fast-food franchising, and she knew what that entailed. But it was as if a bolt of lightening hit both of us at the same time. She remembers the impact of the conversation so vividly:

*We knew we had to record everything we had done in one location, refine the process so it would be fool-proof, document everything, and train others to do it the same way in other locations.*

*My employer, at the time, a commercial real-estate developer, had visited the camp for a few hours one afternoon that same week. When I returned to work the following Monday, he called me into his office and made a proposal.*

*He asked a few questions about our future plans for Royal Family KIDS Camps and added that he could sense our frustration of not being able to take it to a higher level of development beyond only one camp. He indicated he could give me three months off because a project I had been working on was awaiting permit approval. I could use those months to write the training and operations manuals we would need to train other Camp Directors to duplicate the camp model. Then he told me it would be paid time off, using funds from a future bonus incentive tied to the project I was working on. For me, as someone who likes to write and to document procedures, it felt as if someone had laid a gold brick in my hands.*

Those manuals, though continuously updated, are still in use today for training new Camp Directors. Help had come from an unexpected source.

In November 1990, two months after we left the position at the church to launch Royal Family KIDS as a full-time ministry, the first big test of our faith came. One evening, the engine on one of our cars became totally disabled on the freeway as I returned from a speaking engagement. We had asked God to give us one or two more years with our cars so we could avoid a car payment during our first two years away from the church. But God had a plan to teach us faith and strengthen our belief that He really wanted this ministry to continue — a story we now share with all new Camp Directors to help build their faith.

We had been praying for a vehicle and had priced a van but had determined it was out of the question. In January, a businessman invited us to dinner and presented us with a set of keys to an Astro van. Not just any vehicle, but a *van*! It was a perfect vehicle for our needs in this growing organization. An unexpected source had supplied us with a vehicle.

Our first offices were in the two spare bedrooms of our home, and our warehouse was the garage. After two years, we needed to add an additional office person. The two bedrooms were a bit more provincial than the image we wanted to portray, and we definitely had no room for a third person in our "offices."

By November 1992, we began to pray about office space, and a board member suggested that many non-profit organizations are given space in vacant office buildings. This seemed to us like something that happened only to other people.

A phone call later came in February 1993 from a longtime friend who believed in the ministry to abused children. He told us he had rented a warehouse with two offices in front, but he didn't need the offices and all the warehouse space. He offered to donate the space to us and invited us to come look at it. After looking it over, we assured him it would move us beyond our humble beginnings in the back two bedrooms of our home. We eagerly accepted his offer. The building was painted white with purple trim — the Royal Family KIDS colors! How could this be? It looked as if we had planned it that way.

Now we had offices and warehouse space, but we had no shelving to store everything in this big open warehouse. We left the meeting at the offices, and I went on to meet with another friend who owned a manufacturing business. While waiting for the owner to join me for lunch, I asked the secretary where we might purchase shelving. She showed me their newly designed warehouse and offered to give me four pallets of metal shelves they had just removed from their old warehouse.

In less than an hour we had offices, a warehouse, and shelving to fill it — with extra shelves left over. Again, God had moved people, and help had come from unexpected sources.

We also learned that God not only provides from unexpected sources for your dream, but He also brings you the right people at the right time to execute the plan. God provides the right counsel for the right people to help along the way. It was in 1986 that our Camp Grandpa and Grandma, the McNutts, said with tears in their eyes, "Wayne, other churches need to do this." But in order to have the dream, to multiply this program, the entire structural organization had to change. No longer could I be the Camp Director. Instead, God had already placed His hand on the shoulder of the next Director. He was being prepared to handle that responsibility. God brought the right people at the right time. I handed off the "scepter" to my successor so the dream could continue to the next stage of development.

Since then, of course, we have placed the dream into the hands of many Camp Directors who attend a week-long institute. There are also those in local churches who want to reach out to the children. These Camp Directors and Counselors in turn give up a week of vacation and innumerable hours for preparation to make RFK camps a special week for needy children.

Although we have gone through some struggles, God has been faithful every time. One year at our Akron, Ohio camp, they were all set for camp and had completed interviews, training, etc. They didn't have Counselor alternates but they had enough Counselors for the campers they had committed to. At that point, one of the female Counselors received a letter that she had to start her Masters Program earlier than she had planned. She had to start the week of camp. The Camp Director's daughter-in-law had only helped with setup, but stepped up and said she would fill in as a Counselor. She had already been through some of the training with the Director's son and the rest was on video, so she was quickly brought up to speed.

Not only was she a great Counselor, she knew fluent Spanish

which she learned in Bolivia. This opened up a new opportunity for accepting more kids because they now had a Spanish speaking volunteer. God knows what He is doing. He gave us a Spanish speaking Counselor in Ohio to fulfill more of the dream.

As all Camp Directors would agree, it is difficult to find just the right Camp Counselors. However, some times God sends an angel to help us out in times of need!

The Sunday before camp training began in Missouri, a member of the church congregation asked if she could come to training to see what was included and to decide if this was something she wanted to do in the future. Since she had recently adopted one of the campers, the Director knew her motives and decided it might be an opportunity to gain a new Counselor in the future. She did attend training and gave rave reviews about what she had learned about Royal Family KIDS camps. However, what she and others didn't know was that one of the Counselors did not show up for training and backed out as a Counselor when she was contacted.

The Director was frantic in knowing that two little girls would not be attending camp that year because there was no Counselor for them. As tears came to his eyes, he remembered that the adoptive Mom had attended training. Because she had recently adopted, she'd already been through background checks. All that was needed was an application form from her and to ask if she would have the time to attend camp that week. As he dialed her number, his heart raced. As he told her the situation and asked the important question, he held his breath. Yes, she could work it out! God had sent an angel so that two little girls could attend camp! He gives the means to achieve the dream.

Remember, if it is God's dream, He will bring the right people at the right time. And these people will be dear to you. We have friends who go with us to ball games, who pray with us, who go to lunch with us. We have friends who hold us accountable in our spiritual lives. But we have no more exhilarating relationships than with the friends who have ministered alongside us to advance and accomplish God's dream. God brought people who are willing to risk and learn, to pray and hurt, to see the pain of children and administer the medicine of God's love. Counselors, staff members, prayer partners, donors — they all come from unexpected sources. Only the hand of God moves the right people to become involved.

In March 1993, God brought into our lives another person who was moved by the needs of abused, abandoned, and neglected children. He was instrumental in securing a substantial grant that would take off some of the financial pressure that is so much a part of a young, rapidly growing organization. We realized later that he had become the "angel" that one of our friends had prayed for on the eve of our farewell from Newport-Mesa Christian Center in 1990. Again, help came from an unexpected source and from the right people at the right time. And it continues to come, week after week, from faithful friends who give and who pray.

The fifth step in making dreams come true is this: *The dreamer has setbacks and frustrations.* We can look through Scripture and see the life of Paul and Moses. When it comes to setbacks, they had their share. So did Joseph. Our camp in Missouri was full of setbacks and they thought they were not going to be able to fulfill the dream any longer. The Camp Director told the story, which is just one of the countless oppositions faced throughout the years. She wrote:

*After holding many camps, our 14th one almost didn't happen. However, the Lord stepped in to help us.*

*After 10 years at the campground we were using for Royal Family KIDS Camp, we had become comfortable with the owner of the privately owned campsite. In January of each year, we had made a deposit on the campground and we made some final plans with the owner. However, on this particular cold and snowy January day, I had an uneasy feeling as I walked into the campground office.*

*As the owner greeted me, I felt a chill in the air. Unfortunately the chill was coming from him and not the weather! He proceeded to explain that the campground was for sale and, therefore, closed permanently. I couldn't believe my ears! The words "closed permanently" kept echoing in my ears. Why hadn't he contacted me? What about our standard reservation agreement? What would I tell my church?*

*I tried to explain to him that all the campgrounds around us would already be reserved. I begged, I pleaded but to no avail. The campground was closed. I sobbed as I walked to my car and drove home. In a few days I was to leave on a mission trip abroad and I knew others would have to help find another place. As I prayed that our fourteenth camp would take place, I also asked God for His help — for the children.*

*While on the mission trip, my husband contacted every campground, college, university, every place we could possibly use. Meanwhile, I was praying several times a day for guidance and help for him in finding a campsite.*

*Upon my return from the mission trip, I discovered that we still did not have a campground. Now it was February and the chances of finding one were becoming slimmer. I decided to go back one last time to plead my case with the campground owner.*

*As I walked in the door, I could tell by the look on his face that he knew exactly what I wanted. The first thing he said was, "It's still permanently closed." I asked him to hear me out. From previous conversations I knew he was a Christian man. Hopefully he would realize the children we would be hurting by not being able to demonstrate God's love in a safe place.*

*Reluctantly, he agreed to one last year! As I drove home smiling all the way, I thanked God for all the blessings over the past years and promised Him we would continue our mission to help the abused, abandoned, and neglected children He led to us.*

In Iowa, the Camp Director told me that despite all the setbacks and frustrations that they must go through to put on camp, God always makes sure it is the best week they have ever had, year after year. Without fail it just keeps getting better. No matter what the enemy throws their way it just keeps getting better.

The dreamer must understand that setbacks and frustrations, misunderstanding and ridicule will always be part of the process. But experience teaches the dreamer to embrace the opposition and find in the middle of the frustration this principle: God is using the opposition to further the dream. This step begins to mature the dreamer. It forces the dreamer to focus on the dream and not the circumstances.

Through all this, we reach the sixth step: *The dreamer is changed by the dream.* I am not the person I was in 1972, beginning the first Sonshine KIDS Camp for the children of Newport-Mesa Christian Center and the community. My heart and life have changed as a result of moving with God. God has changed my heart and opened my mind to the cries of the unfortunate children who have been made victims by adults. More than 3.6 million children are abused and neglected because some adults use power instead of love.[1] One woman in three is molested before 18 years old. One in four men is sexually molested.[2] One in six men are molested, beaten, abused, or neglected before they turn 16 years old.[3] These lives can be destroyed by abuse, or they can be redeemed by love. That's what we do at Royal Family KIDS — focus on the redeeming power of God's love.

Several years ago, Diane and I had been driving for nine hours when we reached Prescott, Arizona, the site of Arizona's first Royal Family KIDS Camp, with 27 children. We had gotten lost going through the mountains, and we finally thought we had found the camp. We turned onto a dirt road, not really sure where we were. There ahead of us, we saw a woman with two young girls, one on her right and one on her left, each one holding her hand. Diane said, "That's our sign: one adult for every two children. It's becoming a hallmark of Royal Family KIDS Camps." We both looked at each other with tear-filled eyes as we realized the dream had been duplicated in yet a third location, and our lives were being changed and guided more and more by the dream. The dream continued to change us as it became more evident to us that this was more than a simple ministry led by two people.

And the dream continues to change us every day. I asked a young boy at the camp how he felt about the week. Without hesitating he looked up and said, "This must be what heaven is like." Hearing responses like that changes me. It makes me want all the more to provide a safe harbor for children battling the waves, winds, and storms of life.

God is still walking the balcony of heaven, looking across this earth to find people in whom He can plant His dream. Royal Family KIDS camps was the dream He gave to Diane and me. And we hope and pray that the dream He gives you might be to reach out to abused, abandoned, and neglected children too, either through Royal Family KIDS camps or through some other means.

Dreams become reality. When you dare to dream, you will find the means! Never doubt it.

# CHAPTER FIVE

## *Royal Family KIDS Camps: One Week to Change a Life*

If the decision had been ours to make, we would have filled this book with photographs of the battered and abused children we know — not photographs of their bruises or their blood or their crying faces twisted in pain ... but of their happy smiles at summer camp, their faces lit up with joy as they make crafts or play games, their eyes lifted toward heaven as they sing songs and do the hand motions. Those photographs, more than almost anything we could say to you, would convince you that these kids deserve our help. There's nothing like seeing a genuine grin on the face of a girl or boy who had almost forgotten how to smile.

Unfortunately we can't fill this book with pictures of those children because most of them are in the foster-care system of the state where they live. We had to change their names in this book to tell their stories, and to preserve their confidentiality even further, we can't let you see the pictures of their precious faces. But we can describe for you this fact: For many of them, the happiest week of their entire year is the week they spend at Royal Family KIDS Camp. We want to tell you about RFK because it is an example of how some people who care about abused kids have made an incredible impact in their lives. These people are usually not psychologists, doctors, or public lobbyists but ordinary people like you and me.

## Royal Family KIDS Camps

The very first RFK Camp was sponsored in 1985 by Newport-Mesa Christian Center in Costa Mesa, California. I was on staff with the church, and as I see now, God had planted a dream in my heart to reach out to help children whose lives had been devastated by abuse, abandonment, and neglect. That dream became reality.

During that first week of camp, the needs of the children touched the hearts of all of us who worked at camp. We realized that if other churches got behind a program like RFK, we could reach hundreds of abused children every year. So we began to challenge other churches to follow this simple model: Organize a one-week summer camp for abused children in your area. Child-protective agencies and foster families are eager to send children because abused, abandoned, and neglected children miss many normal childhood experiences.

To demonstrate the family concept for children whose families have been horribly broken, we try to create a family atmosphere. Each RFK Camp includes on the staff a Grandma, Grandpa, an Aunt and an Uncle. Their roles are simply to love the children, affirm them, tell them stories, and, of course, to have a heart big enough to be broken many times before the week is over. Children warm up quickly to gray hair and a sincere hug. Before long, they are pouring their hearts out to Grandma and Grandpa. For many of our children, these are the only grandparents they will ever know or with whom they will ever have contact.

In addition to the normal recreational activities of summer camp, each week of RFK is designed around a biblical teaching that challenges the abused or neglected child to draw close to God. For instance, one standard curriculum for camp focuses on Joseph. Can you think of any biblical hero to whom abused kids might relate better? Joseph was injured by his own family, cast into a deep pit, and sold into slavery. A foster child knows and understands how Joseph felt when he was abused, removed from his home, and forced to live in a foreign land.

A lot of these children have been forced from their home and now are living in group homes or with families they do not know. They spend their lives in one home after another and deal with the issues of abandonment and rejection again and again. Therefore, we design our camps to help abused children recover by addressing the very issues that are most important for them.

For instance, one of the worst results of child abuse is children's loss of self-esteem and their feeling that something must be wrong with them to have brought this abuse on themselves. The Cambridge Graduate School of Psychology recommends that abused children be given activities that they can successfully complete to build confidence. At RFK, the activities and sports are all designed to help children do well and feel good about their performance. Counselors and other staff members reinforce good effort, teaching children that they are good and worthy of love and care.

We want the children to understand that they're not worthless, that in God's sight they are precious. Abused children feel like losers before they have even begun to play the game. It's important for us to help them realize that they are winners!

There are no losers at Royal Family KIDS Camp, just royalty. We believe that Jesus sees them as royalty because they are joint heirs with Him. Ever since we have made this our motto, God has been faithful to remind us we're on the right track: when we see the fruits of His vision right before our eyes.

We make every child feel special, right down to playing a big part in teamwork events.

For example, in 1998, Diane saw a demonstration of multi-colored hand bells and sensed in her heart that our campers could *do* this. God had used this demonstration to empower a dream within her heart. She recalls:

*I bought two sets and stored them in the supply cupboard at the office, not resolving how this could best happen.*

*Eight years later, in 2006, someone else hundreds of miles away sensed the same thing. As we sat observing a morning chapel time during a Directors' Training class in Florence, Alabama, the Lord flooded my heart with joy. Mary Lynn, the Music Coordinator, got out a multicolored set of handbells and gave two minutes of instruction to 35 wiggly, excited, noisy children. She handed out the bells and allowed every child to experience "instant success" as the notes of Amazing Grace filled the auditorium of the University of North Alabama's campus (one of our "alternative" camp facilities).*

*More than the success of ringing a bell at precisely the correct moment among many other jingling, clanging bells, was the sheer joy on every child's face. Their wide smiles accompanied every opportunity to ring their bell at just the right moment. Tears streamed down my face as I realized an eight-year dream I believe God dropped into my heart.*

"Success" to these children is a black hole, needing many deposits of this kind to overcome the devastating lack of these moments throughout their childhood.

Now bells ring out in 25-30 Royal Family KIDS camps across the country every summer. What music to God's ears!

Nothing shows children how special they are as much as the feeling of being needed. Ringing that bell at that appointed time gives them a sense of self-worth. It provides a little joy in the midst of the chaos they deal with on a daily basis. It gives them a feeling of safety being able to participate in an event and not getting yelled at or scolded in the process. It revives their hearts!

Abused children often suffer a loss of trust and the anxiety of never feeling safe. At RFK they meet caring Christian adults who can be trusted and by whom they are cared for. One year Laurie came to camp wearing about six layers of clothing; she refused to take off any of her clothes because dressing in several layers had been her only defense against her father's sexual advances and inappropriate touching. Laurie had a boy's haircut, and she did her best to appear to be a rough-and-tumble tomboy in an effort to discourage men from taking an interest in her.

Laurie's Camp Counselor assured her that she didn't need to wear all those clothes all the time, but Laurie wouldn't even change clothes with anyone near her. She continued to dress in layers until halfway through camp, when she finally realized that no one was going to hurt her. One night she decided she would put on her pajamas for bed. As she appeared in the dorm in a pink nightgown, she said to her Counselor, "See, I really *am* a pretty girl."

It speaks volumes that a child like Laurie felt safe enough to let down her guard with her Counselor and friends at RFK. In ways like this, the camp staff tries to rebuild the trust of children who have been abused.

Another problem that many abused children may suffer is an inability to interact with their peers. Constant attempts to hide abuse can make them unable to relate to their peers in a normal way. Plus, they often cope with a conscious feeling that they aren't normal, which can make them afraid to reach out to children they perceive as normal. Royal Family KIDS camps address that problem by helping children develop caring relationships with each other.

Jill, who holds a Master's Degree in Social Work and who is a caseworker for a nonprofit agency in her state, has worked as a Camp Counselor. She wrote to us:

*One thing I have noticed about older foster children is that they usually have seen or know each other. When they see another child familiar to them, they usually say, "Were you at Orangewood?" (Orangewood is a facility in Orange County, California where children initially go when removed from crises.) Or sometimes, it's, "I think I know you." But now for some of the older foster children, that question is changing to, "Weren't you at Royal Family KIDS Camp last summer?" These children are making their own special clique from their camping experience. It's wonderful to see how RFK is making an impact on the children's friendships and relationships with others, even outside of the camp.*

### One Week Makes a Difference

We have no doubt that one week at Royal Family KIDS camps can change the life of an abused child forever ... if for no other reason than the fact that they are introduced to God, a loving Father, whose healing love is the most important ingredient in successful living.

That is the most important mission of Royal Family KIDS camps: to let the kids know that they are God's children.

In Chapter Two you met Carey, whose abusive father had committed suicide after murdering Carey's nine-year-old brother and trying to kill his seven-year-old brother and Carey. Five years after his father had tried to kill him, Carey had become morose, withdrawn, and sad. Terrible nightmares haunted his sleep, and he couldn't conquer a bed wetting problem. After his first week at RFK, Carey's mother noticed a remarkable change in her son. He came bounding into her room, wanting to return to camp again the following week. When she asked him why he enjoyed camp so much, he said, "Because up there *everybody* loves me!"

Three months later Carey's mother told me, "You'll never know what your camp has meant to our family. Carey is like a new child! He used to be sullen and withdrawn. These days I've heard him bouncing through the house, *singing* the songs you taught him at camp."

This is what Royal Family KIDS camps are all about. We are helping children rise above their surroundings and escape the cycle of abuse. We help a child create a positive memory every day. A child just like Ariel. She contacted our offices about the difference a week at camp made in her life. Ariel writes:

*When I was seven years old, I was taken from my birth mother. My mother was not able to care for me due to her mental illness, which debilitated her. At that point in my life, I had been malnourished, uneducated, unloved, and abused. Looking back, I know that someone was watching over me. If God had not interceded, I could have ended up in a far worse place. While I was still in the foster care system, at age 10, I attended a Royal Family KIDS Camp. That one camp I attended in 1991 changed my life in a positive manner. It was there that I witnessed Jillian, a guest speaker who was a singer, abandoned and abused when she was a child, with whom I could directly relate! I accepted Jesus into my heart that week at RFK, and began a new life of love, acceptance, healing, and gaining a family of my own. This journey of healing and giving back is all due to the genuine love and support from those who love me.*

*I left the camp that week, and the abuse did not stop, but the difference on the inside of me never stopped because I knew God had a plan for my life. After living in various homes after being taken from my mother, and nearly adopted, I was placed in another unloving home. But, before it could get any worse, the Lord interceded again, and used my foster mother (from a previous foster home) to intercede on my behalf. After four years in the foster care system, I was finally adopted at age 11, by two loving parents who gave (and still give) so much of themselves to better my life, and allow me to be a part of theirs. I thank God for them in my life.*

*In addition, many people in my life since that time have impacted it tremendously: my husband, son, family, friends, mentors, music and choral groups, and Royal Family KIDS Camp.*

*Today, I am married, have a son, and continue to be immensely blessed by the compassionate, unconditional love, and amazing person in my dear husband, and my sweet loving son. Just before getting married, I earned a college degree, and started my own business helping children with special needs.*

*I have had several occasions at which to share my testimony to Camp Directors, Counselors, and volunteers for Royal Family KIDS camps. It is a blessing and honor to be a part of such a wonderful cause, and help further the truth of God's love and compassion for His children in need. At this point in my life, my plans are to possibly have another child or adopt, and pursue a master's degree. Until then, I am learning, growing, and constantly living thankfully for the wonderful people and blessings in my life and for the one week that made a difference.*

One week not only makes a difference in the lives of foster children but also in the lives of those children "barely hanging on" in their natural parents' homes. Let me share with you a phone call our camp in Geneseo, Illinois, received one morning from a social worker about Susan.

The social worker said, "I heard you have two openings for girls at Royal Family KIDS Camp. I have this girl named Susan who really, really needs to go to camp. It would be so good for her."

The family was poor, but the parents suffered from depression and were unable to take care of their children's needs emotionally or physically. The parents cared very much for their children, but because of their mental illnesses, they couldn't function as parents. All of their children were involved with the law in some way or another.

Their home was so bad that when Susan got to school some of the other children saw a cockroach come out of her backpack. Now the other kids made fun of her. This girl just lived a shabby life, and she knew it. Susan had told the social worker, "I want to be different than all of this. I am going to do something good with my life."

There was another girl named Stephanie who had been taken away from her mother at the age of seven. She was taken away because of physical and emotional abuse along with neglect. She was placed back in her mother's care at the age of 10 and then taken again at the age of 11. At that time she and her mother had been living in a car.

A counselor helped her come to RFK. Stephanie recalls,

*I first attended in 1997 when I was nine years old. I remember thinking I was so happy because I was away from my foster family for a week. From that first year, my life began to change and I attended for three memorable years.*

*RFK didn't just affect one area of my life; it affected every area of my life. I was raised going to church but it was never anything more than a place to get candy for memorizing my memory verse, which I usually forgot when I walked out the door. At RFK, seeing the love that all the staff had for me even though they didn't know me, I was amazed. I watched the dramas and I began feeling God's tug on my heart. I remember the song "I Will Change Your Name," and the words to that song changed me. While I was singing that song, I quietly asked Jesus to change my name, and He did. After that week, I have never been the same. The past has been erased and I have been walking in a new life since the first week of camp. That one week changed my life forever.*

*I went back last summer and was a Counselor leading children to the same peace I found so many years ago at RFK. It was wonderful to see the campers grow throughout the week. It was a very rewarding experience that I will repeat next year. I am now in college and hope to study abroad in Europe. I never would have been able to have these dreams and future if I hadn't been changed in that one week at RFK. Keep doing what you are doing, helping abused, abandoned, and neglected children. I am living proof that it is working.*

Royal Family KIDS Camp is a place of change. We take abused, abandoned, and neglected children and point them in the right direction. In one week, they go from abuse to royalty. We do not simply tolerate them, we celebrate them! You would be surprised how much difference is made in only one week.

### Side Effects

Another positive result of Royal Family KIDS camps is that some staff members choose to become foster parents. Already numerous couples who have served as Counselors at various camps have attained foster-care status. These couples are also exposing the people in their churches to the needy kids in the system, hoping to inspire other couples to become foster parents. There is an urgent need for foster parents, and caring Christian families are some of the best possible places for foster children to learn of God's love for them.

Take the story of Jerry and Glenda Jay for instance. Jerry is a Camp Counselor and Glenda is an Assistant Director at one of our 155 camps. One week after their last camp, they started the paperwork and went to the first introduction class to become foster parents. Ten months later, they were the foster parents to two lovely young girls they met at RFK Camp.

As beautiful a gift as that was for the girls, what Jerry and Glenda had really wanted was to adopt them, permanently. Here is how they tell the story:

*We discussed adopting the girls on the Friday night of the last day of camp. We went to DHS and asked about the girls and about the adoption process on the Tuesday after camp. We found out then that the parents' rights had not been terminated and the girls were not up for adoption.*

*We were not going to give up because a termination hearing had already been set. So we did all the Foster-to-Adopt paperwork and went to an introduction meeting that same week for people interested in foster care or adoption. This meeting had already been scheduled a few weeks earlier, but we just happened to be at DHS and found out about it that same evening. We started the required training classes three weeks after camp. (There just happened to be a training class starting the month after camp.)*

*These classes are not offered on a continual basis, only when there are enough people interested to fill a class. The training required eight days (Saturdays), eight hours each. So, within three months, we attended all the required training classes, got CPR and First Aid certified, had two personal studies and two home studies done, purchased and remodeled a house and moved.*

*We had just sold our five-bedroom, three-bath house and farm two months before camp. And the rented house we were in did not have the required square footage in the bedrooms for four children (our original two children and the two girls). So, along with everything else, we were also house-shopping. We found a house the first week in October, made an offer and closed on the house the third week of October. This house just happened to be across the street from the school we wanted the girls in, which is near to impossible to find a house in this school district. The house needed some remodeling on the inside. So, while we were attending our last couple of classes and going to counseling, many people from our church worked on the house. It was incredible, like something you would see on TV. People brought meals and ladies from the church fixed up each bedroom specifically for each girl; they designed them to be like their rooms at RFK Camp.*

*We finished the house enough to move in and had the first home inspection the Saturday before we got the girls. The second home study was done the same weekend they arrived. They were supposed to come just for a visit that weekend, but on the afternoon we were to pick them up, we found out they would not be going back to the group home they were in. They were ours to keep! Three and a half months after camp we had our girls living with us. We still had to go through all the court hearings and monthly visits and more home studies, but they were with us. It was required they had to live with us six months before we could adopt them. They have been a great addition to our family, and it was all made possible by RFK Camp.*

Another young couple from Oregon had been childless for many years and had decided to pursue adoption. They had purposely steered clear of foster children because they were afraid there were just "too many problems" with them. They volunteered to be Counselors at the local RFK Camp, however, and went through the first full day of training. During that training, they were taught about the four types of abuse, and the "portrait" of an abused child. The trainers emphasized these are just children, and we should not look at them as "damaged," but look at their potential.

At the end of the day the young wife said, "I feel the fear of foster children has been lifted from me today. I see them in an entirely different light now." There were tears in her eyes many times during the training, and she knew God was touching her heart. However, she didn't realize how much.

She and her husband went home, contacted children's services in their area, and told them they were open to adopting a foster child. They now have a beautiful 18-month old girl in foster care, and are in the process of adopting her. They now say, "We would never have done this if it hadn't been for the RFK training we attended."

That experience was just one more confirmation that God is in the business of rescuing these children and reviving their hearts through RFK.

Another example of God's hand in our camps is the story of Erica. One of our Camp Directors from Texas recalled,

*It was Wednesday afternoon, and we were all in the cafeteria. The campers had all been seated, and I was the last staff member to get my tray. I was walking towards a table, and I was confronted by an 11-year-old girl named Erica.*

*She blocked my path and proceeded to tell me the following: "I have been here three days, and I decided that I want you and your wife to adopt me." I was completely caught off guard. I told her that I was overwhelmed and honored that she would choose my wife and me, but it wasn't that simple. She said, "I know. But by Friday I want a YES or NO." She then walked away.*

*My wife attends camp, as well, and that night I told her what happened. I told her I was still overwhelmed. She said, "We spend all week telling our campers about God's Love and God's plan for them." I thought about that, and I prayed for wisdom on Friday afternoon. Once we returned to the church on Friday, I approached Erica and I told her I felt blessed to have met her. I told her that I could not simply say "yes" or "no" because it was not my decision. I reminded her that God had a plan for her life and only He could determine the answer. I made a promise to her that I would pray for God to reveal His plan to both of us if I was to be part of the plan.*

*Two weeks later I received a call from one of our male Counselors. He had been on vacation since camp and he wanted the number for our contact at Child Protective Services (CPS). I asked him why and he said he spent his entire vacation telling his wife about Erica and how he wanted to adopt her. I did not tell him of Erica's and my conversation, but I told him to take some time and pray before contacting CPS. Several weeks later he called me again. He had contacted CPS, and Erica was coming to spend the weekend with his family. A couple months later she was a member of their family.*

*Today, she is 17 years old, a big sister to three other children and loving life. God did have a plan, and he used Royal Family KIDS to bless Erica with a loving family.*

These stories happen at all of our camps. So far, we know of more than 40 children who have been adopted by our Counselors, and we have seen over 150 kids enter the foster care homes of our volunteers; however, we are sure there are many more.

### Be a Part

Not everyone will feel called to become foster parents as these families have, but you can do *something* to help abused children. You don't have to be an expert. You just have to be a compassionate person who cares for children.

"Because a great door for effective work has opened to me, and there are many who oppose me," Paul wrote in 1 Corinthians 16:9. The door is wide open for bringing abused children an example of God's love. Thousands of them are in group homes and foster homes throughout our nation, and they need the Lord's loving touch through individuals. There are indeed many adversaries, for we believe Satan enjoys abused children's pain and thrives on their broken hearts. But we can overcome the adversaries, revive the hearts of children, and can change their lives forever.

When the four stretcher-bearers in the account recorded in the Gospel of Mark arrived at the house in which Jesus was teaching, they faced many adversaries; they couldn't even get through the door. But they didn't allow that to stop them, because they wanted to bring their sick friend to Jesus. The four men dug through a roof to do it. Let's be willing to work as hard for the broken and battered children who need our help.

Becoming a Royal Family KIDS camp volunteer opens the door of awareness to child-abuse issues. But many Counselors and Staff members want to do more throughout the year.

In Poulsbo, Washington, volunteers from Christ Memorial Church became interested in setting up an Adopt-a-Social-Worker program in their community, providing year-round response to very practical needs that a social worker might encounter — supplying a bed, a dresser, a bicycle, needed clothing, etc.

In Puyallup, Washington, the Camp Director, Merrilee, became the "shopper" for the Director of the Child Protective Services, shopping for clothing items that would be distributed to needy children within the Director's jurisdiction — a much-needed helping hand in this overloaded position within the Child Protective Services agency.

Royal Family KIDS is a thriving example of how the Church can make a difference in the lives of children who have been battered and abused. When individuals volunteer for RFK, it not only changes children's lives, it changes the volunteers' lives, as well. You can't be around these wonderful children without being changed on the inside. When you see their tears of sadness turn into tears of joy, it melts your heart and changes your life.

If you are someone who wants to make a difference and you want to know what you can do to help, you can help us through sponsorship. Your giving can help us make sure these children have a place where they can escape for one week out of the year —

it will change their lives forever. You can sponsor children to come to a camp, or you can even launch a camp in your area through your local church.

The lives of abused, abandoned, and neglected children are waiting on someone who cares to reach out to them. Reach out with a gift today and help us reach children who are in need.

If you would like more information about these camps or if you are interested in launching a camp, please go to our website at www.royalfamilykids.org or call/write us at Royal Family KIDS, 3000 W. MacArthur Blvd. #412, Santa Ana, CA 92704, (714) 438-2494.

# CHAPTER SIX

# *Heartwarming Keepsakes and Moments: Memories to Last a Lifetime*

One evening in July 1993, Diane replayed the video of our September 16, 1990 farewell celebration service from Newport-Mesa Christian Center, where I had served as Senior Associate Pastor for 18 years. The purpose and emotions were rekindled as she played the video that strengthened her heart ...

*I heard once again the words of the emcee and our longtime friend in ministry, Dr. Byron Klaus, as he summed up the evening: "What we have seen here tonight is an Ebenezer. We have created a 'memory stone' to remind you of where you have come from and to say that 'hitherto, God has helped you' and that he will continue to be your help and guide."*

*I had been searching for an opening thought for a presentation to encourage women's groups to supply funds for "memory bags" for the campers. We would need more than 700 memory bags for all the campers by the summer camping season, at a price of approximately $31.00 each.*

*That was it, I thought. Ebenezer!*

*In 1 Samuel 7, we read of Israel's encounter with the Philistines and Samuel's fervent prayer for God to deliver them from their dreaded enemy. In answer to Samuel's pleadings, God sent thunder and confused the Philistines, routing them throughout the hillsides, giving Israel a lasting victory.*

*In response to God's action on Israel's behalf, Samuel took a large stone, set it up in the camp, and named it Ebenezer, saying, "Thus far has the Lord helped us" (1 Sam. 7:12). For generations as the people traveled past that stone, it reminded them that in that place, God had revealed Himself and helped them. Samuel created a memorial — or a memory stone — to remind the Israelites of a place where God had miraculously met them.*

*When I heard Byron's words on the video, it was as if God said, "This is what you do for the children of Royal Family KIDS for one week out of their year. You are meeting the deep needs they have for genuine love, trust of adults, affirmation, and the knowledge of a God who loves and will never leave them. They may be hearing it for the very first time in their young lives."*

Whenever we think of "memory stones" or Memory Bags for the children who come to RFK, we think of children like Serena. She attended one of our camps in Arizona.

At the end of the week of camp, the children were brought back to the church where their parents were awaiting their arrival. It's almost a scene of pandemonium! Goodbye hugs from Counselors ... foster families reunited ... show and tell of all the things that happened at camp ... perhaps even a few tears too ... hustle and bustle fills the parking lot. The buses were unloaded. The cars were packed up. Everyone, including Serena and her foster mother, started their journey home hoping that nothing had been forgotten.

Their home is across the valley and they were almost there.

But then, Serena realized she had left her Memory Bag at the church.

With an utter sense of urgency, Serena pleaded with her foster mother to take her back to the church immediately.

Her foster mother encouraged Serena that they would go and

get it later. Serena persisted and wouldn't back down. She insisted that they go back. Getting her Memory Bag back was way too important!

"You see," Serena exclaimed, "all my notes from Counselors and campers from the week, my photo album, my tape and Bible are in there."

Serena continued, "I need them because that is what my week was all about, and I want to have them to remember camp."

With a heart-felt request such as that, who could resist the earnest look in her little eyes?

Serena's foster mother turned the car around and they went back to the church. By that time the camp staff was in the fellowship hall of the church, enjoying some food, fellowship, and debriefing from all that transpired during the week.

As the camp staff began to share, they were interrupted when Serena's foster mother walked in, explaining what had happened with Serena's Memory Bag.

The entire staff was in tears that day as they listened to Serena's foster mother share the story and show her genuine appreciation for all that the staff had done to make such a difference in the children's lives.

That duffel bag had become a memory stone, an Ebenezer for Serena. We wanted each camper to have a Memory Bag, a keepsake of a life-changing week. The Memory Bags contain six items that the campers cherish from the week at camp:

- a Royal Family KIDS camp T-shirt
- a child's, large print, color picture edition of the Bible
- a story-theme Activity Book
- a photo album of personal photos of their week at camp
- a CD of songs sung during camp
- a camp water bottle sipper

Each sponsoring church tries to provide every camper with two T-shirts, one when they arrive so they are all treated equally and look like their peers, and a second one on Friday morning so they return clean and fresh for the foster parents who meet them at the bus. One of these T-shirts is part of the Memory Bag. These T-shirts are more than souvenirs. They are pieces of clothing for children who often come to us with very few clothes in their wardrobe. This is one way we can act on Christ's words in Matthew 25:35-36: "For I was hungry and you gave me something to eat, I was thirsty and you gave me something to drink, I was a stranger and you invited me in, I needed clothes and you clothed me...."

As one of our Counselors was helping her two campers put their clothes away shortly after arriving at camp, she noticed that one young girl had only two pairs of panties to put away. Thinking that perhaps the girl had left another suitcase or bag on the bus or out in the parking lot, she asked the girl, "Did you bring any more clothes? I see you have only two pairs of panties for the week."

Her camper answered, "No, this is all I brought. But it will be OK because if I turn them inside out the next day and wash them out the next night, I will have enough for the whole week."

Already at the age of eight, this girl had learned that if she was going to survive in life, she had to learn to take care of herself. We learned her mother was stoned on drugs and alcohol every morning, and this young girl was already assuming the caretaker responsibilities for the younger children in the home.

Royal Family KIDS camps minister to children not only by providing clothing for their bodies but also by providing a Bible, containing the words to revive their hearts. For most campers, the Bible they receive in their Memory Bag is the very first copy of the Scriptures they will ever own. They ask, "How much will this cost me? These are very expensive. You're going to *give* me this as a gift? What do I have to do for this?"

We wish you could see the faces of some of the campers light up when their Counselors underline a Scripture verse that explains the biblical meaning of their name. Imagine the delight when a boy named David or John sees his name in God's book rather than hearing it at the end of a string of curses or four-letter words. Counselors report that some campers experience a deep inner change after they see the value of their personhood in Scripture.

One camper couldn't be persuaded to put the Bible away after discovering that she could read and understand some of the verses. She was consumed with the joy of having something of her very own and proceeded to carry her Bible around the camp. One Counselor found this young girl reading her Bible *at the same time* that she twirled a hula hoop around her waist.

The third item each camper receives in the Memory Bag is a story-theme Activity Book, which contains the curriculum that accompanies daily chapel stories. The curriculum exposes children to scriptural role models with whom they can identify and tells the stories in language unhindered by Christian jargon.

Tammy Berg, our Camp Director from Bellingham, Washington, and another staff person were intentional about personally driving out to Aaron's home to pick up his application for camp. The year prior, Aaron almost missed camp and they were determined to not let that happen again.

The excitement and joy that Aaron expressed as Tammy's car was coming up the driveway was not able to be contained!

Aaron came running out to the car, jumping up and down and calling Tammy's name — he was so happy to see her! He also wondered if Robby was with her. Robby had been a Counselor in Training the year before when Aaron came to camp. How great to know he still remembered Tammy and Robby from camp!

Aaron grabbed Tammy's hand and took her into the house and over to the living room couch. He proudly lifted up one of the cushions to reveal his flannel blanket that he received from camp the previous year. One of our volunteers, Faye, buys a blanket for every child and Aaron was quick to show off his prized possession from camp!

"I keep it nice and safe here during the day and I sleep with it at night," he told Tammy.

Then, Aaron scurried around the house and ran to his bedroom. With him, he brought back his RFK Memory Bag — filled with the music tape, his t-shirt, his photo album and a few projects that he had done the previous year.

"Look!" he exclaimed. "I still have everything!"

A bag of cherished and precious keepsakes for Aaron — a camper who almost missed camp.

In an article titled *Seven Ways to Optimize Your Brain and Your Life*, Dr. Daniel G. Amen wrote: "The thoughts that go through your mind [i.e. positive memories], moment by moment, have a significant impact on how your brain works. Research by Mark George, M.D. and colleagues at the National Institutes of Health demonstrated that happy, hopeful thoughts had an overall calming effect on the brain, while negative thoughts inflamed brain areas often involved with depression and anxiety. Your thoughts matter."

We try to put together some of the missing pieces of the campers' childhood, giving them special memories to carry through life. Looking at their treasures from camp can revive the children's hearts and fill them with joy all over again.

The fourth item in each Memory Bag is the "Memory Book," a photo album used to help abused, abandoned, and neglected children gain a sense of self-worth. Most children who come to RFK have no visual record of their lives. When the police came to remove the children from their home because of family violence, for instance, the last thing the children stopped to take with them was their baby album or report cards, or baseball-card collection. Even if they would remember to take these valuable memory makers, children in several counties would have these things taken away from them and stored until they would leave the foster-care system maybe 10 or 15 years later (and that's only if these items had been moved with the children from foster home to foster home).

Social workers tell us that for many of the children, Royal Family KIDS camp is the *only consistent thing* in their lives, the only thing they can count on year after year. They long to come back. Social workers also report that the children bring out their camp photo albums at each of their regular visits, carefully retelling their experiences from camp and naming the camp personnel in each picture.

Pictures can be worth a thousand words and a thousand memories too! Sometimes, the children who come to camp don't have any memories of birthday parties ... no clips of being in a school play ... no pictures from opening presents on Christmas morning. Children just like Abby come to cherish the memories of camp.

A foster mother told one of our Directors, Jeanie Estepp, about the time when it came for Abby to be moved out of her home. The two of them were packing up Abby's belongings and reminiscing. Abby didn't have any pictures of her family.

As Abby was gathering and packing her pictures from camp, she told her foster mother, "I have to put these pictures in a safe place." Abby didn't want anything to happen to her photos — they were too precious!

With the utmost tenderness, Abby and her foster mother carefully wrapped the pictures from camp in a shirt and tucked them away between her clothing so they would not be ruined or lost.

Things that we give them at camp are some of the only positive childhood memories that they carry with them from home to home. A gift shows them that we care enough to help them make memories and provides them with items they can cherish for a lifetime.

One student, in particular, from the Seattle area had a distinct reputation for his learning limitations. He qualified for Royal Family KIDS camp as a foster child.

This particular year, each camper received a purple nylon duffle bag as their Memory Bag. Like many of our campers who have so little, he adapted his Memory Bag to be a book bag for the first day of school and carried it proudly into his classroom that morning.

His teacher, taking quick note of the unique "book bag," greeted him and added, "Did you get to go to Royal Family KIDS camp this summer? I, too, went to a Royal Family KIDS camp, but it was another one in Washington." This child, usually downcast and dejected in countenance, suddenly righted his shoulders and stood erect and responded with a broad smile, "Then that means you and me, we got God in our hearts, don't we?" The teacher said it was as if he discovered he had a comrade, an ally, and they now shared something in common. She reported that his reading skills improved remarkably, and throughout the school year he was a different child.

What are the odds that THIS child would be placed in THIS classroom with a Royal Family KIDS camp volunteer? Does God care immeasurably for these children? He surely does. We could share a dozen stories just like this — not coincidence, but by God-ordained connections for our campers. And when, on Friday of Camp, we promise Counselors and Staff members that God will be faithful to place these children in the path of another caring, loving, Christ-like person, He proves Himself faithful.

Music also plays an important role at Royal Family KIDS camp, so we include a fifth item in each Memory Bag: a CD of the songs the children learn at camp. Most of these children do not come from Christian foster homes or group homes, and much of the music they listen to is anything but good for them. We give the children a new song to sing, as Psalm 40 states, and the new song revives their hearts, and brings healing to their soul.

We put songs on the CD that will build their self-confidence and let them know who God wants them to be in this life. One of the songs that has become the all-time favorite song of our campers was discovered in the Fall of 1993 when we were invited to Bellevue, Washington to speak in a Sunday evening service.

During the worship portion of the service, the words to a new song (to us) were projected on the screen, and this most beautiful song began to resonate:

> *I will change your name.*
> *You shall no longer be called:*
> *wounded, outcast, lonely or afraid.*
>
> *I will change your name.*
> *Your new name shall be:*
> *confidence, joyfulness, overcoming one,*
> *faithfulness, friend of God,*
> *one who seeks My face.*
> (Song by D.J. Butler, Copyright 1987 Mercy/Vineyard Publishing
> Administered by Music Services)

Diane remembers every detail. This song changed the course of RFK.

*Instantly, Wayne's and my eyes locked. I was reaching into my purse for a pen and paper to write down the songwriter's name as it appeared on the screen plus the words to the song. At the same time, Wayne was reaching into his vest pocket for a pen and note card to do the exact same thing. Without a word spoken, we both knew instantly that God had just provided this song for our campers, but never dreaming how important these words would become to the children.*

Today it is a staple in all of our camps and the campers are so fond of it they sing and even perform sign language to this incredible song.

These children identify with "wounded" — being hurt deeply, both physically and emotionally; "outcast"— from their home, at school, in their community; being "lonely" — for a family, their pets, their friends, not fitting in to their living situation, or "afraid"— they know fear in its most very real sense — their lives are steeped in fear! This song is like a healing salve to their very soul. This became very deeply impressed on us when we heard the following story.

One of the little boy campers was given the opportunity to perform in a talent show at his elementary school following camp. To think one of our campers had the courage to put themself in front of an audience is, in itself, a real stretch for most of them! And what song did he sing? "I Will Change Your Name."

It could almost be called "The Royal Family Anthem." When we are hurting, God brings solace, revives our hurting hearts, and brings healing to our wounds through music, just as it did for King Saul, in times of anguish and rage, when David played his harp. Our campers thrive on music that reaches into their souls at a deep level, brings peace, and calms their wounded spirit.

In addition to this wonderful CD we also give children a camp water bottle sipper in their Memory Bags. Christ tells us to give a cup of cold water in His name. We take that seriously at Royal Family KIDS. Most of the camps are held in mountainous or desert areas. The children's bodies often are underweight, and they easily become dehydrated. The children play very hard all week, so we provide campers with a water bottle sipper to make sure they drink water continually throughout the day. This, too, becomes a reminder of special memories of the week.

In 1996, as we were conducting a Director's Training Class in Winston-Salem, North Carolina, I was walking through the campground one afternoon. A little girl ran up to me and tugged on my arm and asked, "Are you the guy who can make decisions about this camp?"

I shrugged my shoulders and said, "I guess so. What decision do I need to make?"

"Well, if you would put the words to the camp theme song on the back of this water bottle, we could sing the camp song all day as we go around the camp! Could you make the decision to do that?"

"That's a GREAT idea. I think we can do that."

In about as much time as it took to make a call to the office in California, that decision was made. And in 1997 (12 years after we started Royal Family KIDS), the RFK Theme Song words appeared on the back of the camp water bottle sippers. Many companies pay big dollars for consultants to think of those things! We need more advice from campers like that!

**Memories That Never Fade**

A Camp Counselor named Paul told us the following story. It was the night before the campers would leave, and the "separation factor," as we call it, had set in. Some campers had become withdrawn or sullen, and some of them had become very demonstrative in their behavior; none of them knew how to say good-bye graciously. Most likely, their separations in life had always been hurtful and full of pain, and they knew they must face another separation from someone they had become close to during that week.

As Paul was tucking his two campers into bed, James began to plead with Paul to take him home. Paul was trying to explain to James that he had a job, that he wouldn't be able to spend much time with him, and that he had a family to care for. Paul said to James, "But even though I'm not with you, Jesus will be with you. He will never leave you, James."

James looked up at him with tears in his eyes and said, "Yeah, Paul, but I can't play catch with Jesus. I can play catch with you."

For one week, Royal Family KIDS Camp Counselors present abused children with a real, lifelike Jesus who can play ball, hold hands, and shoot the big water guns. And this new friend never loses his or her temper, never cusses, even though the child may cuss at him or her. These adults become Jesus walking in flesh and bone, and they leave an incredible impression on the children's hearts.

The children can't take their Counselors home, but they can take home the tangible items they receive in the Memory Bag. We are creating memory stones so that one day, many years later, these children will look back at their weeks at Royal Family KIDS Camp and remember the hope that was rekindled and how their life was changed after that week.

We have distributed thousands of these bags, but we really learned the impact they have on these young lives on March 14, 1994. We invited a former camper named Jason to pray at the invocation for our annual fund-raising banquet. Jason was no longer Jason Baxter, who originally came to camp extremely hyperactive, disruptive, unable to learn and totally unaware of the world around him. Jason had been our first camper to be adopted by a loving, Christian foster mother. He was now Jason Baxter Howell.

He was 17 years old and studied several hours each evening to keep up his grades. This is the same Jason who came to camp a hyperactive boy who chewed up his shirt sleeves and was unable to learn.

As we listened to Jason speak, we knew we were hearing about a miracle. Jason said, "Pastor Tesch, you just never know how far God is going to take your idea because you started something like Royal Family KIDS camps for kids like me."

Jason Baxter Howell prayed this invocation at our banquet:

*Dear Lord, I thank you for this very special gathering of people who care for your children who are so precious in the kingdom of heaven. I thank you that we can gather to recognize what Royal Family KIDS is all about.*

*Lord, I also thank you for providing such loving Counselors that help make these camps possible for your children, children who so very badly need to see Your love in practice. Lord, thank you for the very loving environment that Royal Family KIDS has provided for the hurting children. I also ask that you will bring up godly men and women out of the Royal Family KIDS Camps so that they will continue the work that camp planted in their hearts.*

*I thank you for the difference that this camp has made in my life and for the many memories that I have. In Jesus' name, Amen.*

Jason put a memory stone in place for us as he prayed this prayer.

Over six years of attending camp each summer, Jason had received all of the items that are now contained in a Memory Bag, and he still has many of them today. Jason has returned to camp as a Counselor, earning his five-year pin, and is still involved today. For Jason and for hundreds of other campers, positive memories made at camp are for life.

Each year our friends and partners provide a portion of the Memory Bags for new camps. We would love to have your help providing them for next year's new camps. With your gift, you will help provide a lifetime of memories for children who have been abused, abandoned, and neglected. You can put a smile on the face of a little child that has almost forgotten how to smile. You can be a part of reviving the hearts of countless children by becoming involved. Contact us at: Royal Family KIDS, 3000 W. MacArthur Blvd. #412, Santa Ana, CA 92704, (714) 438-2494, www.royalfamilykids.org

# PART TWO:

## How to Revive a Heart: Practical Help for Victims of Child Abuse

# INTRODUCTION

## *The Church:*
## *A Roadblock or a Resource?*
*By REV. DAVID W. DELAPLANE*
*Founder, The Clergy Committee*

In the previous pages you have walked with Wayne and Diane Tesch through the exciting development and expansion of Royal Family KIDS. But Wayne and Diane's concerns reach farther than their own ministry, as exciting and healing as it is.

They are also eager to see believers and pastors, indeed the entire body of Christ, learn more about the tragedy of child abuse, abandonment, and neglect. They want to see Christians become a vital resource in ministry to this need. They long to see the Lord's people fulfill the assurance of the psalmist as applied to abused, abandoned, and neglected children: "Though my father and mother forsake me, the Lord will receive me" (Ps. 27:10, NKJV).

I first met Wayne Tesch in the coffee shop of the San Diego Airport. As I ate marginal airport food for which I had paid "captive audience" price, I was paying no attention to either the food or the price. I was experiencing one of those spiritually charged times as I shared the meal with this unassuming yet dynamic Christian man whom I had just met.

In our work, my wife Anne and I have traveled across the country educating religious leaders on crime-victim issues, seeking to identify and encourage faith-based victim-assistance programs and ministries. Thus it was that I found myself on this day in this busy airport terminal with this remarkable person. Wayne had agreed to accommodate my schedule and meet in this transient arena to share the story that had touched my heart and Anne's more profoundly than any other victim-assistance venture we know.

It has been said that unless you are prepared both to have your heart broken and to be moved to action, do not have lunch with Wayne Tesch. I bear personal testimony to that statement.

I liked what I heard Wayne say about mobilizing the Church to respond to the needs of abused children. For too long the Church has been a roadblock instead of a resource. We deny the reality of child abuse: "It doesn't happen in my congregation." We can be defensive: "I don't want anyone to know what has occurred in my Christian home or church." We sometimes assist the offender at the expense of the victim; this is particularly true if the abuser is active in the church. We can even blame the child victim for "not being obedient" or for being "seductive."

However, the Church is increasingly becoming a valued resource. The next chapters of this book will outline ways you can elevate ministry to abused, abandoned, and neglected children to an important mission for God's people. The prophet Jeremiah lamented, "Since my people are crushed, I am crushed; I mourn, and horror grips me. Is there no balm in Gilead? Is there no physician there? Why then is there no healing for the wound of my people?" (Jer. 8:21-22, NIV).

The following chapters say, "Yes, there is a balm in the Gilead of abused, abandoned, and neglected children as the body of Christ becomes their healing agent." As you read the challenge for individual Christians, pastors, and the Church as a whole to become involved in healing the scars of wounded children, open your heart to learn how God may want to use the gifts He has given you.

## CHAPTER SEVEN

## *Sexual Abuse of Children: A Silent Despair Behind Closed Doors*

Over spring, Jillian was placed in a mental health facility for behavior problems. After all that she had gone through in her short life, it's understandable why: She and her two siblings were locked in a small room for weeks — with nothing to eat, and no place to use the restroom. They were so desperate for food that they ate pencils. They later escaped through a window and were eventually caught by the police stealing food from a local store.

The police officer witnessed the condition of their house when he brought them back — it was appalling. At that time, Jillian and her siblings were removed from their home and placed in foster care.

Jillian and her siblings were also the victims of sexual abuse a silent killing despair too atrocious and repulsive to even describe. Their father victimized them in ways that degraded them and stole their innocence.

But, thankfully, the story doesn't end there. Jillian and her siblings have all attended RFK camp. Their hearts have been revived, and the healing from their atrocities has begun. Through camp, Jillian felt safe, secure, and valued by her

Camp Director, Heidi. A trustworthy bond was established and Heidi was able to help Jillian make it through the tough times ahead. She wrote Heidi a letter expressing her thanks:

*Dear Heidi,*

*Thank you for praying for me. It has really helped; I am back on track. Thank you all! I'm glad I got to see you again. Well, I was having a rough time in the hospital. You made me feel good yesterday by talking to me. It was special to see you. Thank you for letting me go to camp for free!*

*Love, Jillian*

Child sexual abuse is an insidious form of abuse that is felt with more shame and treated with more secrecy than any other form of abuse. It is perpetrated by family members, as in Jillian's case, and also by pedophiles and child molesters who are not part of the victim's family but who may be close friends of the family.

The scope of child sexual abuse, whether in the home or perpetrated by strangers, is incredible. Some estimates indicate that one in ten families in the U.S. is involved in sexual abuse.[1] The average victim is nine years old, although children still in infancy have been abused. Although in the case of incest the incident is sometimes one isolated act, it is more commonly a pattern of abuse that typically occurs within a long-term, on-going relationship between the offender and victim. It escalates over time and lasts an average of four years.[2] Sexual abuse is one of the top three reasons that children run away from home.[3]

Studies show that 80 percent of runaways and homeless girls reported having been sexually or physically abused. Thirty-four percent of runaway youths (girls and boys) reported sexual abuse before leaving home, and 47 percent of runaway youths (girls and boys) reported physical abuse before leaving home.[4]

Over 70 percent of runaway and "throwaway" youth in 2002 were estimated to be endangered, based on 17 indicators of harm and potential risk. The most common endangerment component was physical or sexual abuse at home or fear of abuse upon return.[5]

The children who have escaped the prison of abuse are left roaming the city streets trying to find love and affection. If we don't reach out to these runaways, they will be running all their lives from an enemy they will never escape. If we do not reach out with arms of love and hearts of compassion, these children will become another nameless statistic. It is time for us to heal the wounds and revive the hearts of these children.

## Sexual Abuse

Sexual Abuse is the horror no one wants to talk about! In spite of the apparent widespread occurrence of child sexual abuse, it is probably the most unreported form of abuse — for a variety of reasons. In the first place, societal taboos foster denial and non-recognition. Also, a child who has been sexually abused frequently will not exhibit the outward signs that expose other forms of abuse. Finally, sexual abusers of children are the ones who go to the greatest lengths to assure that this is "our secret"; therefore, victims of child sexual abuse are least likely and least able to report what has happened.[6]

Because many incidents go unreported, complete information on child sexual abuse and abusers is not available, but the best research shows several facts about this crisis:

- Victims of child sexual abuse are usually not "attacked" by a stranger. Generally the perpetrator is well known to them: a parent, a relative, or a family friend. Studies show that 73 percent of reported sexual abusers say they knew their victim before the first incidence of abuse.
- 38 percent of perpetrators were a friend or acquaintance of the victim.
- 28 percent were an intimate person (close association or familiarity).

- 7 percent were another relative.[7]
- Child sexual abuse perpetrated by someone known to the child usually is conducted in the home of the victim or the abuser.
- Child sexual abuse perpetrated by a stranger usually is conducted outdoors in warm weather.
- In many cases coercion is not required in order to molest a child. Rather the perpetrator has won the trust of the child through affection or gifts, and the child allows the molestation without protest.
- Most child molesters say their adult sexual orientation is heterosexual.
- In cases of pedophilia, as opposed to incest, most of the victims are boys abused by men.
- The majority of known child sexual abusers are men.
- Girls are the most frequent victims of child sexual abuse.[8]
- Although some people believe that only very attractive or "seductive" children are at risk or that molestation happens only to children in "bad" neighborhoods or children who are improperly supervised, sexual abuse may happen to children of any age, whether beautiful or plain, whether they live in good or bad neighborhoods, whether they are properly supervised or terribly neglected.[9]

One recent study focusing on adult female rape victims found that nearly 30 percent admitted to having been raped before they were 10 years old. More than 30 percent were raped when they were between the ages of 11 and 17.[10] This is a statistic that should awaken our senses and call us to action as human beings. Wounded hearts and crushed spirits must be revived and healed.

### Incest

Incest has been cited as the most common form of child sexual abuse. Research indicates that over 10 million Americans have been victims of incest.[11] Studies show that about 46 percent of all reported child sexual abuse cases involve incest.[12] However, because intra-familial child sexual abuse is the least likely kind to be reported, this figure is probably very understated. The most common form of incest is between father or stepfather and daughter. About nine out of 10 reported cases of incest involve young girls rather than young boys.[13] The perpetrator is not always someone who "looks" like a child molester or who obviously drinks too much; the person can be a church leader or an astute businessperson.

A variety of reasons have been suggested for why some men sexually use their daughters or stepdaughters. As with most abusive parents, sexual abusers often were physically and/or sexually abused as children.[14] They may also feel insecure with themselves and their ability to handle the stresses of marriage and fatherhood. A father who feels this same way may respond in one of two directions: rigid authoritarianism or passive dependency. In either case, incest may result.[15] The authoritarian type will feel more in charge if he can subjugate his daughter sexually. The dependent type will substitute the easy target of his daughter for a normal sexual relationship with his wife, demanding that his needs be met as if he were the child.

Another contributing factor to the onset of incest between father or stepfather and daughter can include the daughter's role as the central female of the house when the mother is absent or not able or willing to assume this role.[16] The daughter then may be seen as the "little mother" of the household and is open to abuse by the father or stepfather who places her in the role of his "little wife."

In some cases the wife and mother may be aware of the incest but is unable or unwilling to stop it. In such a case the mother may see her daughter as a rival for her husband rather than as the abused victim of a sick person.

If you are a mother who suspects or has reason to suspect that your husband or male friend may be abusing your daughter, you *must* do two things:

1. Find out. If you're ignoring telltale evidence because you're certain that your husband or friend would *never* do that, then you may be allowing the child you love to suffer terribly. Ask your daughter or confront your husband or the friend. If you are mistaken, you'll be relieved. But if you are correct, you must report the abuse and save your child.

2. If your husband or friend admits the abuse but is remorseful and promises that it will never happen again, *don't believe him.* Your caution has nothing to do with your love for him and everything to do with protecting your child. Report the abuse to the proper authorities, and insist that the offender see a counselor who can advise you whether or not the man can remain in your home and keep his promise not to touch your daughter. In the meantime do not allow him to be alone with your children, even for a minute. If the counselor determines that your husband or male friend will abuse again, then he must go live somewhere else while he undergoes therapy and attempts to overcome this problem.

It is very important for your daughter's self-esteem to remove the offender rather than remove your daughter from your home. Help your daughter understand that what happened to her was not her fault. It was the abuser's fault, and he has to leave until he works through his issues. If you send your daughter away, not only will she feel that she is being punished and internalize the blame for this incident, but your abusing spouse or friend probably will turn his attention to other children in the home.

Other types of incest, including father-son, mother-son, mother-daughter, and sibling incest are not nearly as common as father-daughter, so less research has been devoted to them. However, any child sexual abuse has the potential for profoundly devastating the child as well as the family.

## Pedophilia

In North Carolina, one man was convicted of 99 counts of rape and other crimes against children; 148 counts against the same man had been dropped before the trial. He had been the owner of a day-care center. The children's parents had *entrusted* their children to him and his staff.[17]

Child sexual abuse such as this, which is perpetrated outside the family, is often the work of a pedophile, someone whose sexual orientation is directed toward children. Pedophiles prefer children as the objects of their sexual gratification. These are the "stranger danger" people we warn our children about, but it may not always be a stranger who threatens our children, as the North Carolina incident illustrates. What can you know about pedophiles, and how can you protect your children from them?

Most pedophiles are men. Although females can be pedophiles, it is very rare. Pedophiles plan their lifestyle to gain access to children. They may even marry in order to get close to the children of their new spouse. They are often the "special friend" of the children they abuse. For instance, they may give the children presents, take them on outings, or invite them home with them. Pedophiles may invest weeks in grooming their intended victims, gaining their confidence. Pedophiles may also use pornography or child pornography to desensitize the intended victims, showing them that other children do these things and enjoy them.

Pornography plays different roles in child sexual abuse. Many pedophiles use pornography to teach victims how to perform sexual acts. Others take pictures or videos of their victims not only for personal pleasure but also for trade with other pedophiles. Photographs and videos may also be used to blackmail victims; the abuser may threaten to show the bad pictures to parents or to have them published in the newspaper if the children tell what has happened to them.

Pedophiles themselves claim that 20 million American men

are sexually attracted only to boys.[18] These pedophiles will prey on prepubescent boys who have no father figure or adult-male role model. The affection and attention of a pedophile, lavished on a lonely young boy, serve to break down any barriers the boy may have, opening him to the sexual suggestions of the pedophile. Many adult male pedophiles see the Greek tradition of pederasty as a good one and are working to make sex between men and boys legal and accepted in our society through such organizations as the North American Man-Boy Love Association.

## Adolescent Offenders

Recent news reports tell haunting stories of teenage baby-sitters who turned out to be child abusers, sometimes sexually abusing children for whom they were caring. But it is actually not surprising when you consider that studies of adult sex offenders show that their problems began when they were young. Some child molesters committed their first sex offense when they were as young as eight years old; some rapists committed their first rape when they were only nine years old. Another study found that about 35 percent of adult sex offenders had already begun to exhibit behaviors such as exhibitionism and voyeurism when they were adolescents.[19] The most serious and chronic offenders often show signs of antisocial behavior as early as the preschool years.[20]

In the past, adolescents who exhibited inappropriate sexual behavior with other children were generally regarded as merely exploring their emerging sexuality. However, the most recent research shows that juvenile offenders are representing a larger and larger proportion of all sex crimes. Add to this the fact that inappropriate sexual behavior in adolescents seems to precede adult sex offenses, and the problem of juveniles abusing juveniles appears to be a major issue.[21]

Most adolescent sex offenders are male, although female adolescents can also be sex abusers. In their book *Helping Victims of Sexual Abuse*, Lynn Heitritter and Jeanette Vought give an idea of how an adolescent offender may find the opportunity to develop and maintain a sexual relationship with a much younger child:

> *He is typically a nice quiet young man, a loner who keeps to himself. He is usually an average or above average student who is appreciated by his teachers because of his pleasing behavior. He is usually isolated from peers, has low self-esteem, and a history of abuse, usually sexual. Because he does not have friends who take up his time and because he is quiet and well behaved, he is often asked to baby-sit for small children. His victims are usually fond of him and will participate in sexual activities for long periods of time before the secret about the abuse comes out. If the children do tell about the abuse, they may not be believed, because he is such a "nice guy."* [22]

On the opposite side of the coin, some juvenile offenders may use violence and force to abuse children sexually. These offenders often have been violently abused themselves and are trying to regain some control in their lives by overpowering and controlling someone weaker. They also may have a desire to express pent-up anger and to humiliate someone in the same way they have been humiliated.

Children are just as devastated by an adolescent abuser as they are by an adult sexual abuser. If you are concerned about protecting your children from abuse by adolescents, do not allow an adolescent male to baby-sit for your children. Although this sounds discriminatory, it only makes sense when research shows that most child sexual abuse is perpetrated by males.

**Ongoing Sexual Abuse**

In many reported cases children are sexually abused not in one isolated incident but on a continuing basis. The ongoing relationship of the abuser and the abused moves through several stages:

1.  *Engagement*: The abuser gains the child's trust and cooperation through non-threatening, non-forcible means, such as games.

2.  *Sexual interaction*: Sexual activity such as fondling is introduced, but these activities generally build in intimacy and frequency.

3.  *Secrecy*: The child has been engaged in sexual activity, and secrecy is enforced so the perpetrator will not be caught and can continue to abuse the child.

4.  *Accidental or purposeful disclosure*: This step may never be reached because a child victim is often afraid to report the abuse or accepts it as the price of affection and affirmation. Accidental disclosure implies that the abuse has been discovered before either party was ready for disclosure and may precipitate a crisis. Because the victim only then unwillingly discloses the abuse, he or she may not be believed. Unless a child victim receives immediate support after disclosure, the victim will frequently retract and say the story was a lie. Tragically, family members are more willing to believe that a child has lied than that a child was abused.

5.  *Suppression*: Families have a tendency to suppress any publicity or information surrounding the circumstances of child sexual abuse once the disclosure stage has been reached, especially if the abuser is a family member of the victim. The victim may even be forced to recant the disclosure or state that the consequences were minimal — "no harm done."

Child victims of sexual abuse generally feel unable to stop the abuse, especially because the abuser is stronger and older. The victims are forced to "accept" what is happening because they are helpless to stop it. Once victims feel forced to accept the situation, they may also mentally assume the blame for what is happening. Alcoholism, drug abuse, and self-destructive behavior have all been identified as "accommodation mechanisms" developed to help child victims cope with continued sexual abuse.[23]

**Effects of Sexual Abuse**

The long-lasting effects of sexual abuse of children are very similar to the scars suffered by a child abused in any way: loss of trust, anger, fear, and feelings of helplessness.

Victims of child sexual abuse may be more likely to blame themselves and suffer with guilt than would children abused in any other way, in part because society regards sexually abused children differently than any other abused children. Because victims of child sexual abuse are at a physical disadvantage and are in no position to fight back against an adult perpetrator, they may be forced to accept what is happening. This acceptance is sometimes mistaken for consent. Some people blame young female victims of sexual abuse for the abuse because their clothes or their actions were considered to be seductive.

However, long-lasting effects of child sexual abuse can be mitigated. Prognosis for a victim's recovery is especially good if:

1.  *The child is not blamed for the abuse.* If your child is sexually abused, never make him or her feel responsible. Establish right away that all the guilt lies on the abusive adult.

2.  *The child receives the support and protection of family.* It's very important that whether or not the abuser is a family member, the rest of the family members rally around the victim and make him or her feel safe and secure.

3.  *Consequences to the family are minimal.* Child sexual abuse — like any other form of child abuse — must be reported to the authorities when it is discovered, even if the incident occurs within the family. The victim is likely to recover best from the incident if disclosure doesn't disrupt family life violently.

4.  *The family is not dysfunctional.* A healthy home and family

life will help the victim of child sexual abuse recover more readily.

5. *The victim was stable emotionally before the abuse began.* An emotionally healthy child will recover better from the serious effects of sexual abuse than a child who was troubled to begin with.[24]

The sexually abused child has the best possible chance for recovery if all of these conditions are met. Note that some of the conditions need to be met beforehand: providing a stable home and family environment for your child and ensuring that your child is emotionally healthy. These steps will also help to create an environment in which your child feels free to talk to you, helping the child to tell you about a potential abuse situation and perhaps avert a tragedy before it happens.

The next chapter will discuss steps on how to take action to protect children from sexual abuse as well as steps pastors and Christian counselors can take to help victims of child sexual abuse.

# CHAPTER EIGHT

# Rebuilding the Wall: A Model for the Church's Response

Today millions of children are broken, bruised, and emotionally paralyzed because of child abuse. They need strong friends like you and me to work on protecting them and bringing them to Jesus so He can bless them. It is time that we rebuild the wall of protection around the children so that they can be sheltered from these enemies called abuse, abandonment, and neglect.

The model for how to rebuild this wall can be found in the Old Testament story of Nehemiah, who rebuilt the wall around Jerusalem after the Israelites returned from captivity. Just as Nehemiah led the people in restoring their fragmented and bruised nation, the Church can restore hope and life to the fragmented and bruised lives of abused, abandoned, and neglected children.

Let's examine several steps Nehemiah took in rebuilding the wall that can benefit us in our construction. The first step Nehemiah took when he felt God's call to rebuild the wall was to understand the extent of the problem.

## 1. Understand the problem

"One of my brothers came from Judah with some other men" Nehemiah writes, "and I questioned them about the Jewish remnant that survived the exile..." (Neh. 1:2). Nehemiah wanted to get all the information he could about the task he felt called to undertake.

Similarly, when the Church decides to reach out to abused, abandoned, and neglected children, we must understand the problem as fully as we possibly can. The Church must educate Christians on the issues of child abuse. For too long the information has remained covered up. Sometimes the information will be harsh and brutal, but we must not run from the facts or the people behind them just because we are uncomfortable with the graphic details. Graphic stories are the norm for abused children. For 3.6 million kids, physical and sexual abuse and neglect are everyday experiences.[1] Christians can show these children that abuse doesn't have to be "normal." A normal childhood should include security, happiness, and the opportunity to rebuild a life broken by abuse or neglect. However, we as Christians can't help abused children until we understand the facts and support the ministries that currently help abused children. Churches must challenge people to become involved as volunteers or as donors in helping children bruised by emotional, physical, and sexual abuse.

Not only must the Church educate its people about child abuse as an issue, but it also must safeguard its own children against potential abuse. The Church can do this in three ways. First, it can teach body-safety classes aimed at helping children know the difference between good and bad touching as well as helping them know how to protect themselves from molestation. Second, the Church can screen people who will be working with children in an attempt to identify potential abusers. Third, the Church can implement a team-teaching approach in its children's programs. All classes and outings should be arranged so that a minimum of two adults are always present, preferably with one or more of the children's parents in attendance. Appendix D lists several valuable resources churches can use to help prevent child abuse within their church.

## 2. Respond with prayer

After Nehemiah hears the report about the condition of the wall around Jerusalem, he responds with grief and prayer. "When I heard these things, I sat down and wept. For some days I mourned and fasted and prayed before the God of heaven" (Neh. 1:4). Nehemiah passionately prayed to God, asking for His help in rebuilding the wall and restoring God's people to their former status.

Similarly, the Church must respond in prayer to the plight of abused children. The Bible continually reminds us that all great works begin with prayer. The great work of mending the hearts and lives of abused children also will require honest, fervent prayer. Christ himself models this for us. "Then little children were brought to Jesus for him to place his hands on them and pray for them. But the disciples rebuked those who brought them. Jesus said, 'Let the little children come to me, and do not hinder them, for the kingdom of heaven belongs to such as these'" (Matt. 19:13-14).

I can remember arriving at one of our camps during the afternoon and seeing the campers and Counselors swimming and playing in the pool to beat the heat. I saw one shivering young boy cross the deck to Mary, one of our camp staff members. Mary wrapped the little guy up in a fluffy San Diego Padres beach towel. As I watched, I saw the child nestle into Mary's arms, and I saw her eyes close. Mary was praying for the young boy. He found in that young woman's arms the love of Christ. The young boy found not only someone to cuddle him but also someone to give him God's blessings.

You may or may not be in a position to put your hands on the heads of abused children and pray for them, but every Christian in America can remember these kids in their prayers once a day. That in itself will make the heart of the Church sensitive to the needs of the children.

In the New Testament, we see Christ's heart broken with compassion for a widow whose only son had died: "As he approached the town gate, a dead person was being carried out — the only son of his mother, and she was a widow. And a large crowd from the town was with her. When the Lord saw her, his heart went out to her and he said, 'Don't cry'" (Luke 7:12-13). Christ's heart went out to her. His compassion led him to raise the widow's son from death. Our hearts go out to abused, abandoned, and neglected children. We can allow that compassion to motivate us to work to raise them from their emotional death and physical pain, reviving their hearts and bringing life back to them.

### 3. Plan the work

When God called Nehemiah to rebuild the wall around Jerusalem, He also called him to plan how that rebuilding would be done. As it happened, Nehemiah was the cupbearer of the ruler Artaxerxes. Nehemiah needed Artaxerxes' permission to rebuild the wall. Because Nehemiah believed so strongly that God would soften Artaxerxes' heart, he boldly planned out his needs before he even went to ask for the king's permission. When Nehemiah approached the king, he already had a plan.

The Church also must plan how to address the devastating effects of child abuse. Chapter 11 of this book outlines several plans for how the Church can best respond to the crisis of child abuse. As you and your church make your plan, use one of the suggested plans or modify it to meet the needs of your church and community. Every great success story is built on the plans of great minds.

## 4. Pull together

The rebuilding of the wall around Jerusalem is really a tale of cooperative effort. A glance at Nehemiah 3 reads like a *Who's Who* of old Jerusalem inhabitants. Everyone worked together; everyone labored side by side. "Eliashib the high priest and his fellow priests went to work ... The men of Jericho built the adjoining section, and Zaccur son of Imri built next to them ... Meremoth son of Uriah, the son of Hakkoz, repaired the next section. Next to him Meshullam ... made repairs, and next to him Zadok son of Baana ..." (Neh. 3:1-4).

The entire chapter lists all the different people who worked together to rebuild the wall. It serves as a perfect model for outreach to abused children. People from all backgrounds and life experiences can have a strong impact when they work together for God. In order to achieve the dream of helping abused, abandoned, and neglected children, we must all pull together in one mind, in one accord, with one mission. There is no room for division when you are called to a vision. Because where there is division, the vision dies. We must pull together as a church and stand united to help the children of this world.

Because our camps have a ratio of one Counselor to every two campers, each camper gets a lot of concentrated affirmation and support from their Counselor. Craig, a volunteer at a RFK in Arizona, had grown particularly close to one of the boys, Ricky. He wanted to keep up contact even after camp had ended. Craig's wife, Lucy, however, was reluctant. After all, she and Craig were not foster parents; they weren't psychologists; they weren't trained social workers. What could they possibly offer an abused child who had been removed from his home? Lucy doubted whether they had the skills, time, or resources to help anyone.

But Craig persisted, believing they could make a difference in this young boy's life. He and Lucy received the county's permission to continue to see Ricky and to take him on special outings. The opportunity to see and spend time with Craig overjoyed Ricky, who had never had such healthy, wholesome attention from an adult. On one outing Craig noticed that Ricky's shoes were falling apart. The next time he saw Ricky, Lucy had agreed to come along. Together they bought Ricky some new tennis shoes. When Craig and Lucy saw Ricky again, he gratefully said, "I just want to thank you for those new shoes you bought me."

Lucy became a believer that day. Yes, Ricky needed foster parenting, a social worker, maybe even therapy with a psychologist. But he also needed the help of loving friends. Lucy realized that anyone who is willing to give a simple gesture of love or a small gift like new shoes can make a real difference to a kid like Ricky. "Craig, we raised three children," she reflected later, "and I don't think any of them ever thanked us for new shoes."

Working together, we can change the lives of abused, abandoned, and neglected children.

## 5. Face the challenge

Nehemiah knew that he was doing God's work as he rebuilt the wall around Jerusalem, but this did not mean that he did not have adversaries, setbacks, and problems. His response to these challenges was simply to *face* them.

As the Church works to rescue abused children and help put their lives back together, it will encounter problems as well. Like Nehemiah, building the wall, we're bound to come up against troubles. But also like Nehemiah, we're obligated to work through them. Nehemiah's troubles came in the form of two men, Sanballat and Tobiah, who didn't want the wall rebuilt. "When Sanballat heard that we were rebuilding the wall, he became angry and was greatly incensed," wrote Nehemiah. "He ridiculed the Jews, and in the presence of his associates and the army of Samaria, he said, 'What are those feeble Jews doing? Will they restore their wall? Will they offer sacrifices? Will they finish in a day? Can they bring the stones back to life from those heaps of rubble — burned as they are?'" (Neh. 4:1-2)

When we try to rebuild the lives of abused children, we shouldn't be surprised to hear the same kind of taunting arguments from our enemy, Satan: Do you expect to restore the lives of abused children who have been maimed at the most significant developmental years of their lives? Will you finish in a week? Can you bring these wrecked and bruised children back to life?

The taunts were meaningless to Nehemiah, and they are meaningless to us. We *can* revive the hearts and rebuild the lives of broken children, but we must be committed to working through our problems.

As the American Church responds to the needs of abused children, as we join together to rebuild these shattered lives, surely the prophecy of Isaiah is ours. "If you do away with the yoke of oppression ... and if you spend yourselves in behalf of the hungry and satisfy the needs of the oppressed, then your light will rise in the darkness, and your night will become like the noonday ... Your people will rebuild the ancient ruins and will raise up the age-old foundations; you will be called Repairer of Broken Walls, Restorer of Streets and Dwellings" (Isa. 58:9-12).

We can lift the yoke of oppression from little shoulders who never should have to carry it. We can satisfy the needs of the oppressed by giving abused children the wholesome love and affection that all children need. We will be the rebuilders, restorers, and repairers of young lives that otherwise have very little hope in this life. We will face many challenges to our work, but we can be ready to meet them.

When Nehemiah's enemies threatened him with military force, he simply instructed his workers to build the wall with one hand and carry their weapons with the other hand. What a beautiful model that is for us today. With one hand we can rebuild the lives of abused, abandoned, and neglected children, and with the other we can protect them from their enemies.

## Can we really make a difference?

When thoughts like this overwhelm me, I remember two things. The first is a statement by Mother Teresa: "I can't help them all, but I can help some." The second is the hope that God graciously and lovingly holds out for these children. It seems He almost had them in mind when He inspired David to write Psalm 40. "I waited patiently for the Lord; he turned to me and heard my cry. He lifted me out of the slimy pit, out of the mud and mire; he set my feet on a rock and gave me a firm place to stand. He put a new song in my mouth, a hymn of praise to our God. Many will see and fear and put their trust in the Lord" (Ps. 40:1-3).

Can the Church make a difference? Can I make a difference? Can you? Yes. Yes. Yes.

The children *are* waiting for someone to bring God's love to them. The Scripture says that God turns to us and hears our cries, but for many abused children, their cries seem to be met only with violent acts of anger or appalling sexual or emotional abuse. God does hear them. But He also asks us, His Church, to hear them and to turn to them. Will we lift up abused children from the slimy pit, out of the mud and mire? Will we reach into the closets where they are locked up and the lonely hiding places where they have withdrawn? We must, for we are God's hands extended to this dying world. As we follow His leading, He will set the feet of these children on a rock, give them a new song to sing, and validate their trust in Him.

As you've read, the scars of child abuse are many and deep. Like the tender limbs of a tree, children can be bent only so far before they are broken. But *broken* isn't a frightening word to God; He once was broken for you and me. But abuse can press a little heart until it is crushed. And yet, even the word *crushed* isn't a frightening word to God; He was crushed beneath the weight of the transgressions of the world. But He defeated them.

"I will give you a new heart and put a new spirit in you," God says in Ezekiel 36:26. "I will remove from you your heart of stone and give you a heart of flesh." In self-defense, abused children may develop hearts of cold stone, but God can give them hearts of love. God is able to change forever the lives of these desperate, needy children. But you and I must be willing to help. Working together, we *can* make a difference.

One of our favorite stories to illustrate the point happened along the southern coast of Australia, where thousands of starfish had washed up along the beach and were then drying out and dying in the sun. One frantic young boy raced about among them, picking up the starfish and heaving them back out to sea as quickly as he could. A jogger along the beach stopped and watched the boy in his work for a moment, then he said, "I understand what you're doing, but do you really think it will make a difference?"

The boy looked up at the man and then down at the dying starfish in his hand. "I don't know, mister," he said, "but I think it will make a difference for this one."

We must reach out even if we just reach one. Making a difference in one life can affect hundreds, even millions of people. You never know when you reach that one; you could be reaching the next president, next teacher, next inventor, or next businessperson that will change the world. Truly, one is worth the reach.

## CHAPTER NINE

# *Making a Difference: Unsung Heroes Hall of Fame — Part 1*

When I was a boy growing up in upstate New York, the Baseball Hall of Fame in Cooperstown held special memories for me. I was a young baseball-card collector, and walking the halls of the Baseball Hall of Fame helped me envision awe-inspiring actions on the ball diamond. As an adult, I visited the Basketball Hall of Fame in Springfield, Massachusetts. I shot hoops in a special interactive display and saw the beat-up peach basket that Dr. James Naismith used when he invented the game.

Let me introduce you to another hall of fame.

In 1990 Diane and I sat in the morning service in a Southern California church that had just sponsored its first RFK Camp. The speaker asked all the adults involved in the camp to come forward. As those 40 people stood in the front, the speaker declared, "The people that stand before you today are the unsung heroes of the faith. They are the ones who had the courage and the heart to step into the unknown and come back victors." At that proclamation, the congregation of 2,000 people stood to their feet and applauded these volunteers. As we sat in the back of the church, we looked at the people who surrounded us and saw tears rolling down their faces. God's power was nearly tangible in that moment. Those 40 people could have easily remained anonymous in a church the size of that one, but for one day they were recognized for their sacrifice and service. For all the ones that have received recognition down through the years at RFK, there are so many others that have given tirelessly throughout the years and have not been recognized until now.

We want to share with you some of their stories, and to list here a small fraction of the names that should be inscribed in the Unsung Heroes Hall of Fame.

### Members of the RFK Unsung Heroes Hall of Fame

People who volunteer at Royal Family KIDS Camps and the family of contributors who finance the camps are usually not experts in psychology or child abuse, but they make a wise choice. They choose to follow the command of Christ, who asked us to bring the little children to Him.

We count the RFK Camp Directors, Staff, Counselors, Grandmas and Grandpas, Aunts and Uncles, and donors as unsung heroes. Their names may one day be forgotten, but their heroic deeds will live on in the hearts and minds of children they have touched through their sacrifice.

GLENN GARVIN knows how the children of Royal Family KIDS feel because he has been there. His parents separated when he was a baby, and for a time he was raised by his father, a heroin and cocaine addict. When Glenn was four years old, he was adopted by a different family, but the father of this family was abusive. The marriage broke up, and Glenn's adoptive father committed suicide when Glenn was 12 years old.

"The difference between Royal Family kids and me is that they have been pulled out of the home for their own protection, and I wasn't. But I can relate to their fear and insecurity. My past has given me a lot of understanding for these kids," Glenn says.

"It helps me work more effectively with them."

Glenn was a Camp Director for 11 years in Lakewood, California, and he is now on staff at Royal Family KIDS national office. Glenn is one of our unsung heroes.

Glenn became a hero in 1988 when he met a boy named Jason at our third camp and started something that unknowingly began a Royal Family tradition that is used to this day.

Glenn told us the story of Jason:

*I was walking from the swimming pool up to the dining hall and was talking to my wife about my birthday, which was coming up later in the week. Jason overheard our conversation and said, "Hey I have a birthday this week too!" I asked him about some of his favorite birthday memories. "Was it a special gift or party?" I'll never forget his answer: "I've never had a birthday party." One of his foster brothers was listening as well and he snapped, "You have too. Remember the time they took you to Jack in the Box? That was for your birthday." "Oh yeah," Jason admitted. "I did go to Jack in the Box once for my birthday." I just stood there in shock for a moment. I thought to myself, is it possible that the only recognition for this little boy's nine years of life is a hamburger at Jacks?*

*Injustice began to rise inside me as I reflected on all the disappointments in my past. I didn't experience too many positive memories, but I was determined to create one. I just couldn't allow Jason to go through another birthday without a gift and a celebration. I drove to the local K-Mart and found a watch as a gift for Jason. I told the cashier the story behind the watch. Through her tears she called the manager over so I could repeat the story. The manager, who was also weeping, said, "Just take the watch," and waved me on without having to pay.*

*After returning to camp I told my wife about Jason. She said, "I wonder if that has happened in the other children's lives as well?" I began asking other children about their birthday memories and I found many who had the same story. I even discovered two little six-year-olds that didn't even know the date they were born. Robin came up with a fantastic idea:*

*Let's celebrate everyone's birthday!*

*That was 1988. Now, nationwide, every summer at every camp, we throw a big birthday celebration for all the children at camp. We call it "Everybody's Birthday Party." It's complete with cake, party favors, decorations and Birthday Boxes™ packed with gifts — but most of all we tell them how very special they are.*

Glenn Garvin, you are a hero to these children. You are an unsung hero.

LYNELL BROOKS, a personal friend, served as a camp nurse of the original camp, and later directed the camp sponsored by Newport-Mesa Christian Church. Lynell jokes that she went to lunch with us one day and ended up drafted to serve at the camp! Before coming to RFK, Lynell had worked with us in other camps. She comments on the differences she sees between RFK and other camps: "We thought we knew what we were doing. One counselor for every two campers sounded easy! But working at RFK Camp was the hardest thing I have ever done in my life. I wasn't prepared for the emotional wringer. These children were nothing like the kids at other camps at which I had worked. Along the way somewhere, some adult has changed the course of history for them."

Lynell observed this about RFK campers, "As a camp nurse, I found these kids didn't need much nursing. They aren't used to being 'mothered' every time they have an ache or pain. Other kids come to the camp nurse for every little thing, but RFK kids just tough it out and think they should take care of themselves. Nurturing is so foreign to them."

"The same principle applies to the food," Lynell reports. Usually, kids at regular camps complain about the food constantly. "RFK campers eat it and love it. Many campers hoard the food, stuffing their pockets with food from the table since they often don't know where their next meal is coming from. They have to be reminded that another meal will be served in a few hours."

The first day of camp, when the buses arrive, is Lynell's

favorite part of camp. The kids, Counselors, and Staff are filled with emotion. "When I see them piling off the bus, I can notice how much they have grown. It's heartwarming to watch the kids run to find their Counselors. It's as if they're coming home. For many of the children, we are the only consistent thing in their lives, sometimes the only thing they can really count on."

Like almost everyone involved in Royal Family KIDS camps, Lynell says life is never quite the same after a week of camp. "It opens my eyes to realities I never would have known about. These kids are in our schools and our foster-care systems, and we never know their pain. I feel angry to think how adults can do such horrible things to innocent children. Through working at Royal Family KIDS camps, I have grown more compassionate and aware."

When Lynell's daughter was seven years old, a camper of the same age came to the nurse's office at camp. The girl had been taken from her family and placed in a county shelter because of her parents' drug use. She was new to the foster-care system, a little sick, and very scared. The parallels between Lynell's seven-year-old daughter and this seven-year-old girl struck her. "I just wanted to take this child home, but I couldn't," she says. "We learn to trust in the sovereignty of God as we try to love and care for these children because we don't always have the answers."

Lynell, you and the staff of the Newport-Mesa camp may not have all the answers, but you are heroes!

SANDY HAMLIN did something you've probably done with your children and grandchildren: Sandy took a young girl with an injured ankle to the emergency room. Because she had read the girl's camp application and file, Sandy knew that when this young girl was only three years old, her mother had abandoned her. Sandy understood why the girl screamed almost nonstop when she was placed on the gurney to be taken for treatment. She wouldn't calm down until Sandy had taken her hand and stayed with her the entire time. Afterward, Sandy said, "You were afraid

I would leave you, weren't you?"

The young girl answered, "Yes. My mother did. Thank you for not leaving me."

Sandy didn't start out with much enthusiasm for Royal Family KIDS camp. When her pastor first asked her to be involved, she agreed with reservations. "I guess I wasn't convinced that anything could be accomplished with these kids in five days," she says. "But after the training camp and observation, I came home absolutely convinced. I plan to be a part of Royal Family KIDS as long as I can because it's so important for these children to learn about Jesus' love for them. When I see the expression in their eyes, it makes it really worth it."

Sandy, currently serving as a Camp Director, says her favorite part of camp is Everybody's Birthday Party. The hall is decorated, and a huge cake shines with one candle for every child present. "We let the youngest child blow the candles out," Sandy says. "Most of these children have never had a party before. Because we don't tell the children about the party ahead of time, it's a surprise when they walk into the hall. They are just shocked to think it's a celebration for everybody's birthday."

Sandy's husband and daughter are also involved with Royal Family KIDS today. "Having worked with RFK has changed my perception of my own church. We're a small congregation, but we have really rallied around abused children. We have done a lot with very little."

After 15 years they are still going strong and are still heroes to these children.

For doing so much for the children, Sandy, her husband, her daughter and her church congregation deserve a place in our Unsung Heroes Hall of Fame.

CONNIE HUTCHISON is a wonderful woman from California where she works as a Disabilities Minister. Her oldest daughter was born with Down Syndrome and this is where her work with disabilities first started.

In 1992, she was hired as the first Director of Disabilities Ministry at the First Evangelical Free Church of Fullerton, California. Her job was to identify and break down the barriers that keep people with disabilities and their families from being able to fully participate in the life of the church. In the late nineties, one of the members of the congregation introduced her to Royal Family KIDS and her family's world of disabilities ministry quickly expanded to include children who are in the foster care system due to abuse, abandonment, or neglect.

While attending Director's Training at Canby Grove, Oregon, she fell in love with a little boy with cerebral palsy who struggled to walk due to abuse he received as a baby, a condition called Shaken Baby Syndrome. She vowed that the anger she was feeling would be channeled into positive actions that would make a difference to other kids in the years ahead, with or without disabilities, that could have a life-changing experience at a Royal Family KIDS camp.

She works with wonderful children such as Allen. "Allen has cerebral palsy, ADHD, epilepsy, and a learning disability. He is not an easy camper to have. Allen has severe tantrums, language that would be unacceptable in all homes, and that first year at camp would eat very selective food items, only using his hands. He is not the 'favorite' kid in the group home he lives in during the year and has low self-esteem. No one wants Allen and he senses this. Initially the thought was not to let him come back to RFK the second year due to his oppositional behavior and lack of interaction with the other kids. However, this will be Allen's fourth summer with us and we have come to realize that he needs RFK as much or more than any other camper in our camp and we need him."

Seth is another young boy at her camp with oppositional defiant disorder, ADHD, schizophrenia, and mental retardation. He will be joining them for the second time this summer. As his foster mom wrote on his application, *Seth has been through some rough patches in his short life. This experience will benefit him greatly.* I think that sums it up for most of our campers ... probably in an understated way. Because of great people like Connie and her entire family working with her at the camp, these children are receiving the care they need. Thank you, Connie. You are a hero!

DAN AND BECKY BUHR are Directors of one of our camps in Nebraska. They attended Directors Training at "The Firs" in Washington in 1993. The decision to take that step of faith came nearly three years after Dan received a vision that revealed young children playing, laughing and having a great time in a camp setting. However, in the vision, there was a look of hurt mixed in with the smiles on many of the faces. That was it. After sharing this vision with many friends who agreed to pray for discernment and fulfillment, Dan was handed an article about RFK in a youth activities magazine by a youth pastor at his church. He immediately knew that it was an answer to the three-year discernment process that he had thought about each day since he received the vision.

He decided that he was going to hold a camp, and at his first one he had 24 kids registered and money in hand to cover expenses. All actually came to registration with the exception of three children from the same family — one of those children had misbehaved the night before, and as punishment, the foster family had decided to keep them all home from camp. Becky didn't give up with that response, and after a conversation with their social worker on the phone, all three were brought to camp the next day. One of these girls has now grown up and spent a week as a Counselor in 2007. She is now 19 and on her way to giving back what RFK has done for her and her siblings.

With a congregation of 90, funding a camp has been a struggle. But the Lord gave Dan the assurance that the money would always be there, and it has been for each of the 13 years. The number of campers over the years has ranged between 48 and

64. Nine of the original staff team have served all of the 13 years and some have served at other weeks of RFK within the state as well.

After a few years of holding camps, Dan was asked to apply for the Director position at Covenant Cedars Bible Camp. As a self-employed business owner, with a senior in high school and many other seemingly insurmountable obstacles, the Buhrs laid everything before the Lord, once again asking for His will. As the obstacles began to disappear, Dan was offered the position. He and Becky sold the business, moved to a new community and have now served at Covenant Cedars for seven years. During that time they have been able to assist four more Nebraska camps in the start-up process, three of which are also held at the Covenant Cedars facility. In 2007 the camp facility was host to an RFK Directors' Training Institute as two more Nebraska camps were trained, as well as one from Michigan and one from Missouri. The Missouri folks were actually part of the camp staff in the initial years of the Buhr's week of RFK and are now building a brand new facility in Missouri that intends to host at least 10 weeks of RFK camp each summer in the near future.

Dan and Becky — thank you for all that you have done and keep up the good work. You are heroes!

KEN RHODES AND ALEX. Alex first walked into a Royal Family KIDS Camp with the weight of the world on his shoulders. After being transferred from foster home to foster home, the oldest of four children, he was shouldering the responsibility of being "dad" to all of his siblings. He longed to be a regular kid and do what young kids do, but his family was most important, and he put their needs before his own.

Alex was a caring and generous young man who was mature beyond his years. But he found himself in need of a father figure to help guide him. During his third year of camp, he met the person who would fill this void in his life — his Counselor, Ken Rhodes.

Ken built a special bond with Alex the week he was at Royal

Family KIDS Camp. Ken knew there was something special about this young man, so after camp, Ken received permission from Alex's social worker to visit him and his family. These weekly visits included church, breakfast, holidays, and birthday celebrations. Alex was soon becoming a part of the Rhodes' family. Ken and his wife Kerry were becoming the parents that Alex longed for in his life.

Ken was performing many of the duties of a father, like taking Alex to his little league games. Ken was in the stands cheering Alex on just as a proud father would do. This meant the world to Alex, and Ken began to change Alex's world.

As Alex continued to grow up into a young adult, he never forgot the principles that he learned from his Counselor, Ken. Alex, now 21, has become a great young man, serving in the Armed Forces for nearly four years. His service has earned him one of the Army's most prestigious medals of honor, the "Purple Heart." He received this because of his bravery in battle. He is still protecting lives and putting the needs of others before his own.

Alex is in his second tour in Iraq and plans to enter the police force when his tenure is over. He wants to protect young lives, just as his was protected through the leadership and guidance of Ken Rhodes and Royal Family KIDS Camp.

Alex continues to give back to the camp as he has served as a Counselor. He wants to give back to the ones who gave hope to him. Alex contributes his dedication, goal setting, and caring today to the love and support he received from Ken and Kerry Rhodes and Royal Family KIDS Camp.

Alex knows the difference a week can make. A week can change the rest of your life!

MARK AND GEORGINA HILL from New York became involved in RFK after coming across this ministry when they discovered our first book, *Unlocking the Secret World,* in a Christian bookstore in Long Island, New York. They read the book in two days. They just couldn't put it down and then couldn't stop talking about what they had learned with tears streaming down their faces. At that time Georgina was on staff at the Brooklyn Tabernacle as an Assistant Administrator in the Children's Department. She began sharing over and over again what a strong impression the book had made in her heart and how she was sure she somehow needed to get involved.

She felt compelled to call us!! Something she would have never done within her own personality but she felt compelled to let us know the impact the book was having on her life. Surprising to her, later that day I called her back. Her "tongue was tied" but she told me how the book had made a strong impression on her and how she needed to find out more about RFK.

That was over 11 years ago and since then, they have hosted nine camps, participated on RFK's Cabinet, and have equipped new Directors by participating on the teaching team for RFK. Georgina told us,

*"We have had the pleasure of seeing first-hand the power of prayer from a Godly staff and Counselors. We have seen volunteers give of their time freely to be God's hands extended to the abused, abandoned, and neglected children in New York City. We have witnessed the difference that one week can make when we invest in them and infuse children with positive memories every hour of the day. Royal Family KIDS is the best ministry opportunity I have had the privilege to serve in. The standards are high and the training is wonderful."*

Mark and Georgina, you are two heroes to RFK.

JOHN VAN WICKLIN is a childhood friend of mine who also lives in New York. He says that out of all the things he has done, he is most proud of his involvement with RFK. He and his family work endless hours reaching the lives of abused, abandoned, and neglected children in the central New York area. Since 1995, he has been the Director and Founder of the Houghton, New York RFK.

He is one of the few people involved with RFK who knew me as a child. We attended Sunday School together, and went our separate ways after High School. In 1995 our friendship was rekindled when we saw each other at a meeting. At that time he revealed to me that he named his first son after me in 1970. He stated that he wanted his son to carry the name of a man that has great character and integrity. What a compliment!

The camp he started in New York continues to this day, and so does our wonderful friendship. Thank you, John. You and your family have been faithful in many years of service and friendship. You are heroes to me and to these children.

LARRY AND KIM SPIESS are Camp Directors at our camp in St. Peter, Minnesota. Since 2003, they have been working with RFK. After their first year of camp in 2004, they held their first annual Partners' Banquet to raise money from area businesses.

At the first Partners' Banquet, State Senator Michelle Bachmann was the keynote speaker. A local social worker and RFK advocate spoke at their second annual Partners' Banquet. They experienced moderate success in raising funds through these efforts.

However, in 2006 their church rented out their Family Life Center to the Republican Party of Minnesota for a local caucus meeting in the fall of 2006. Not long after the meeting the pastor received a call from Governor Tim Pawlenty's office. At the end of the conversation, the Governor's representative, Richard Tostenson, asked the pastor if he could explain to him a ministry called Royal Family KIDS. Richard listened intently and quickly caught the vision.

On June 4, 2007, at the third Annual Partners' Banquet for RFK of St. Peter, Governor Tim Pawlenty was the keynote speaker. He spoke about the vision of RFK and the need for this program to reach abused, abandoned, and neglected kids across the nation. Governor Pawlenty also openly shared his faith. There were no political motives involved in the evening.

St. Peter RFK had asked the Governor to lend his support and effort to raise money to start an endowment fund to generate additional camps across the state of Minnesota. From RFK of St. Peter, MN, a new organization, RFK of Minnesota, was born.

The Governor's presence at the event gained them access to many business leaders and influential persons to whom they otherwise would not have had. Because of the event, their camp has been featured on local news stations and in many local newspapers.

With this banquet and the formation of RFK Minnesota they anticipate the opportunity to start two to three camps within the next couple of years. The boldness and vision of the senior pastor and Larry and Kim Spiess, who saw a need greater than that of the local area and took a step of faith to pursue that vision, has expanded dramatically. Thank you for being ambassadors for the vision and for being our unsung heroes.

LEON LO is another young man from California. He got more than he expected when he began working with RFK in 1998. He had been praying for a mate for a long time that shared the same heart for ministry as himself. While at a camp recruiting event in 2003, he met a young lady named Nicole. He saw her and had a chance to work with her during camp and was impressed with how she interacted with the kids. As she would tell him stories about the kids' lives that were being changed, her face would light up. Not long after camp they began dating and continued to work at camps. Today, they have been happily married for four years, and continue to work at RFK, with Leon serving as a Camp Director. You never know what God has in store for you when you volunteer to help abused, abandoned, and neglected children. There's not a better place to meet a wife than being faithful in the place where you are serving. Leon you are a hero!

STEVE LEE, from Arizona, is another man who received this wonderful blessing. Steve first met his wife Jackie when he started working with RFK. In 1996, after their first year of camp she caught his eye. They started dating and discovered they had the same heartbeat when it came to helping children. After they married they desired to have children of their own. However, at the age of 18, Jackie had been treated for cancer and told that she would not be able to have children. So they planned to foster or adopt kids. A short time after they were married, they became pregnant. Isn't that just like God.

They had two children their first two years of marriage, then they agreed to wait upon God's timing to fulfill their desire for foster/adoption. When their children were five and almost six, Steve and Jackie asked them how they felt about sharing their family with a child who needed a family for a while. They each went to their rooms to eagerly clean and prepare to share their room. The Lee family now has fostered one child for almost three years, and another for nearly a year. They hope to adopt these children as God provides. This is what the word "heroes" is all about!

RANDY AND KIM MARTIN are two people from California who have taken this vision to the next step and are inspirations to RFK. What initially began as a one-week service opportunity to "work out" what God had accomplished in their lives, has turned into a vibrant and ever-evolving ministry serving abused, abandoned, and neglected children. Their experiences filled their hearts with compassion and their minds with possibilities and a great challenge.

"Will I go to RFK next year?" turned into, "What can we do on a daily basis to serve these children?" After much discussion, prayer, and research, they developed a Christian faith-based organization that recruits, trains, and supports individuals and churches to serve abused, abandoned, and neglected children. This process eventually led to the formation of Covenant Community Services, Inc. (CCSI).

At CCSI, their mission is simple — "providing love and hope to abused, abandoned, and neglected children." They attempt to complete their mission in the spirit of excellence learned from years of serving at RFK. It is easy to see how the leadership training, coaching, mentoring, and corporate consciousness have impacted the daily operations and organization. They have developed services that have grown beyond foster care to mentoring. They help emancipate youth through housing and support. They provide mental health services, transitional service to children and families, and offer faith-based consulting and education.

When they provide an orientation to staff, volunteers, or potential partners, their story always begins with RFK. It was RFK that had changed their walk with God, their worship to God, and their work for God. Their community is not the same due to the impact of RFK. Young adults have successfully made it through the child welfare system with the help of Covenant Community Services, Inc. What began as a simple response to a request for Counselors at a one-week camp has become a life-long process of providing hope and love to abused, abandoned, and neglected children.

Randy and Kim not only started an organization to help children, they also got involved personally. In 2000, they were able to rescue an RFK camper named Jovan out of the group home system and place him in the home of their RFK "Aunt and Uncle," through their foster care ministry. The relationship between the Martins and Jovan continued to grow and deepen. In 2002, Jovan moved into their home, and they loved him as their son. Jovan remained with their family following his emancipation from foster care and attended the local junior college. Jovan moved out of their home to independence in 2007 at the age of 21.

Randy recalls, *"RFK has done many things for our family, our ministry and life. One of the most amazing gifts that have been received from serving at RFK was a son ... Jovan. We cannot imagine life without Jovan in it and that gift has changed lives and generations. Thanks, Royal Family, for adding Jovan to our family. It is a connection that came in a 'God moment' that changed history."*

Thank you Randy and Kim Martin. We don't know what

RFK would do without such great heroes as you.

TOM RIZZO is a doctor from Illinois who has adopted children as a result of RFK. I first met Tom Rizzo at a church in Minnesota in the late 1980s. I was there talking about RFK. Tom said that he and his wife, Jan, said to themselves that night, "He was talking to us." They looked at each other and said, "We HAVE to do this." They were already involved with foster care, so it only seemed natural that they would also be involved with a ministry to children in the foster care system.

A few weeks later, there was an announcement in the bulletin of a meeting for anyone interested in directing a Royal Family KIDS Camp, so they went. They were the ONLY two people at the meeting. Needless to say, it was a "God thing."

When they went to training in Winston-Salem, they ran into a man named Carlton Milbrandt, whom they later learned was married to a lady named Dyonne from New York, a friend who had meant a lot to Tom as a kid. Tom came to Christ at a youth conference, held by Dyonne's church, when he was in ninth grade.

He started attending that church and found Dyonne was a caring adult who was rock solid in her faith. For years, if there was a potluck or a picnic at church, Tom said Dyonne would tell him not to worry about making and bringing anything because she would make enough for both of them. She became an inspiration to him. Although she was going through trouble, she always was joyful, even during the hard times. Throughout the years, she helped him go on during his tough times, too.

To Tom, Dyonne was a shining example of being "Jesus with skin on." She never made him feel uncomfortable, and always welcomed him with open arms. She is the major reason he is a Christian today. Anyone can be "nice" once in a while, but it was Dyonne's faithfulness that proved to him that Jesus is real.

From that reunion between Dyonne and Tom, to the start of Tom and Jan's first camp in St. Paul, Minnesota, and then moving to Geneseo, Illinois, where they are preparing to conduct their fifth camp, God's influence and guidance is truly evident in the "coincidences" that occur as they prepare for camp each year. At their first year of camp, in Geneseo, they were able to bring 26 children, despite the church's total adult membership being only 24! This past summer, they planned on bringing 38 children.

So you can see that there are many unsung heroes involved with RFK, not the least of whom is Dyonne Milbrandt, and her dedicated husband, Carlton.

I think Tom said it best when he wrote, "If you want to see a miracle, just get involved with RFK. Miracles happen every day at camp, and often during the preparation as well." Tom, Dyonne is not the only unsung hero, you are on that list as well.

## CHAPTER TEN

# *Making a Difference: Unsung Heroes Hall of Fame — Part 2*

John and Jude Hubbell have been a part of RFK for over 10 years. They shared an inspirational story with us that we want to share with you because it is what being a hero is all about.

John wrote,

*It was with much fear and trepidation that we accepted Sam as a camper at RFK. You see it was only our second year of offering Royal Family KIDS Camp and Sam had very special needs. Just two years earlier Sam had been burned over 70 percent of his body. His siblings had filled a dog food dish with gasoline and then lit a match. Sam was burned from the top of his head down to his knee caps. He suffered several head and facial burns and scarring, the loss of fingers and used a feeding tube the first year. Since that time he had been cared for by a wonderful foster family, but even they needed the break that our Royal Family KIDS Camp provided.*

*A child like Sam definitely needed to come to camp, but who could provide for his special medical needs? God provided just the right young man — a medical student who was just beginning his residency, loved the Lord and was eager for the challenge/opportunity. Not only did Sam have to have special meds and lots of sunscreen, but he needed a bathtub for daily baths to keep his scarred skin supple.*

*Sam faced his own psychological issues too. He especially faced the fear of rejection and concern about his physical appearance. In a conversation with another camper, Sam noticed that camper was troubled. Sam asked him what was the matter and the camper responded, "You look like a monster."*

*Sam's response: "I know."*

*In spite of everything, Sam was always a peacemaker among the campers. Our favorite quote over the three years Sam attended was, "Come on guys, knock it off. We're supposed to be having fun here." Sam attended our camp for three out of the five years he was eligible. He only missed the summers when more surgery was needed.*

*His Counselor developed a special bond with Sam and was even allowed to be involved in one of Sam's surgical treatments. Because of this relationship, we would occasionally hear how he was doing and the struggles he had because of his appearance as a teenager. It was a very difficult time for Sam.*

*Each year as the RFK team gathered to get ready for the next camp, someone would bring up Sam's name and wonder how he was doing. We lost contact once his Counselor became an MD and established a practice out of the area. But in the spring of 2005, one of the members of that early RFK team ran into Sam at a local car dealership where he was employed. After greeting each other, Sam told the staff person what an important time camp was for him. Then Sam excitedly shared the news that he was getting married within the next few weeks and moving to Washington, D.C.*

John and Jude, because of the willingness to love and care for Sam, you — and the young doctor who served as Sam's Counselor — are heroes in our book.

TOM TURCO is a man from Idaho who has had the privilege of taking RFK to Australia. In 1995, he asked Sue Carpenter and Carolyn Boyd from Carpenters Cross Ministries to be his Bible

Story teachers. Sue and Carolyn conduct children's camps and children's ministry training in the Pacific Northwest and in Pacific Rim countries, plus Europe. Part way through the week, Carolyn told Tom that she was going to start Royal Family KIDS in her home country of Australia.

When Carolyn returned to Australia to begin the recruitment process to start the camps, she determined the best way to build the support for Australian camps was to send people to be a part of the Boise, Idaho camp. Since Carolyn's camp was to be sponsored out of the missions department of her home church, she encouraged her people to go on a short term mission trip to the mountains of Idaho to work with the abused, abandoned, and neglected children of the Treasure Valley.

Tom anticipated having the eight Australians join him for the RFK he directs. In February of that year he contacted the campground and mentioned the dates of the upcoming camp, which he had confirmed prior to leaving camp the year before. The campground director responded by telling Tom that the dates he had given him were incorrect and that they would have to come in a week earlier. When he advised Carolyn of the change via e-mail, she and Sue immediately called him from Australia to let him know that all eight people had already purchased non-refundable, non-returnable tickets and were locked into the dates that he had originally been given. They closed by saying that they would be in prayer for the situation.

Tom then called the campground director again and pleaded with him to change the dates and allow them to come on the originally scheduled time. The director told Tom that it was impossible and wished him well finding another camp facility. So there he sat on a late Friday afternoon in mid-February without a camp facility, knowing that the camp facilities that would be acceptable for Royal Family KIDS Camp in his area were probably already booked for the week that the Australians were coming. Tom had visions of tents in pastures, renting condominiums, any other sort of accommodation just so camp could go on. He called members of his local team and requested that they start praying for a solution.

In the weeks that followed, Tom was turned down by every camp he could think of; the week he needed was simply booked up. He and his wife discovered one final camp with possibilities and drove out to look at the grounds — but it was dead of winter, and snow on the roads prevented their visit. As they turned back to go home, they noticed a new lodge being built on a previously undeveloped campground. They stopped in and talked to the workmen and found out that the camp was building a new lodge and it was to be completed by the time their camp was to be held. Then, they found out the week they wanted was available! They offered a heartfelt prayer of thanks for God's provision for His precious children and breathed a collective sigh of relief, reminded of the power of the prayers of the Australians and how much God really wanted Carolyn to start camps in Australia.

They didn't know that the next miracle was about to occur. As camp drew near, it was obvious the new lodge would not be finished in time for them to use it. On one particularly rainy day a week before camp, he called the building department to determine if they would be able to use the new lodge, or if they were going to have to rent an "army tent" for their group meetings. The building department agreed to issue a temporary occupancy for the building, which was an unprecedented action. Again, proving to all of them the power of prayer and how much God cares for not only these special children in Idaho, but also the children of Australia.

Presently, Tom's camp is still honored to have Australians come on short-term mission trips to participate. As an additional blessing, several of the people from the Boise RFK have had the opportunity to participate in an Australian camp. Tom, your perseverance and passion are inspiring. You are a hero!

THE SMITH FAMILY has been involved with the Newport-Mesa

Royal Family KIDS Camp in California almost from the beginning. Loretta Smith went to the second year of Camp, and her husband Walt came along the next. They both served as Counselors for several years, and Walt always had amazing stories to tell his own grown children about the boys he had served each year at camp. Then came a "promotion" — Walt and Loretta became the Camp Grandma and Grandpa! They were both gifted in this role, and Walt's special passion was sending notes of encouragement and affirmation. Through the camp mail system, every single child received a personal note from Grandpa Walt.

His Camp Director once noticed Walt staying up all hours to write these notes and encouraged him to get some rest. Walt's response? "I can rest 51 weeks of the year. This is the one week I can give to the kids."

Walt and Loretta always challenged their daughter Valerie to start a camp in Washington state, but Valerie admitted the children who come to Royal Family KIDS Camps scared her. She did not think she had it in her to serve and love them the way her parents did.

When Walt went home to be with the Lord in 1999, we were heartbroken, along with the family. No one could really replace him in the camp. But Loretta wanted to continue serving, even without Walt, and her daughter Valerie bravely pledged to join her mom at Camp, for as long as Loretta wanted to go. Valerie was scared that first year in 2000, right up until she saw the frightened face of the first child get off the bus. Then she knew any fears she had were nothing compared to the fears and horrors that those children knew, and Camp became easy for her.

Her brothers, John and Jeff, were looking for some way to honor Walt's life and legacy. They spearheaded the Walter Smith Golf Classic to benefit Royal Family KIDS. The goals were three fold: Sponsor kids to go to Camp, help new Camps get started and assist Royal Family KIDS with their budget needs.

Other family involvement with Royal Family KIDS grew as John's daughter, Jenne, joined her grandmother at Camp for four years during the time she attended college and was married.

Jeff's church, Seaside Community in Huntington Beach, California, took a hold of the vision when I spoke to its congregation on a Sunday morning. They've conducted camp now for five years. Jeff's wife, Kim, is part of the camp leadership and their daughter, Holly, started as a Counselor in Training and has now been a Counselor for two years.

In Washington, Valerie and her husband, Steve Burnett, were privileged to be the Directors of the first Royal Family KIDS Camp in Eastern Washington. This past summer was its third year. Their whole family is involved, and their son Seth does the video and editing for the camp and is part of the drama team.

Royal Family KIDS Camp is a "language" that the entire Smith Family has learned, speaks well, and is passionate about. It started with their parents saying "yes," and reaching out to children who needed the unconditional love of God. You all are heroes!

MENG AND CAROLINE YEO are Camp Directors in Singapore. Their camp is held in the Marriott Hotel, as there are no camp facilities in the area. They bring the camping atmosphere indoors and still have a wonderful time. They held their first camp in a school, the second in a hotel. For the past three years partial sponsorship came from a foundation. This foundation is from the private monies of a well-known chief executive in Singapore and spouse of a statesman. Meng and Caroline have underwritten the camp's costs themselves and have now turned their first home into an office and a warehouse for RFK Singapore. After running the camp for five years, they have been preparing for the past three years to launch a camp in Japan.

They always believed that children are like flowers; like flowers, they must be "planted" in the right environment. They must be nurtured, put in good soil, and then they will blossom. Hence, they started flower companies in Japan to work on raising funds for Japan's RFK. They do the same thing for Singapore. They have many fundraisers to help support the camp they hold in Singapore. In a country with 4.5 million people, they are reaching abused, abandoned, and neglected children. In a place where they have no real means of water except the rain, they are letting love rain down on the abused children in their country. Meng and Caroline, you are heroes to Singapore and to RFK.

BILL MARBLE is a Dairy Queen (DQ) owner in Ohio and has been involved in RFK for many years. He always states that Dairy Queen and RFK have many similarities: Because of their many different locations and great ideas, they have become a successful system. A new store or camp doesn't have to start "from scratch" since applying the system to a new location will make it work. Each needs to make minor adjustments for their location, but the program always works because it has been established and proven to be effective.

Both organizations have a training school with required attendance before someone can operate a store or direct a camp. Hands-on-practice with experienced teachers makes it look easy, but to accomplish the task at hand there must be teamwork. Dealing with all the different personalities involved is what makes it challenging. The product is great but it must be served with love and care in order to be effective and make an impact.

Seasoned veterans and a core of experience are present to give new people someone to model themselves after and who can answer their questions. Another similarity is that Camp Directors or DQ owners must constantly encourage and motivate. At DQ, employees must give the customers a positive experience so it will make them want to come back. At camp, it's to show God's grace and love to the campers so that, hopefully, the campers will want to know more.

"The major similarity between a DQ and RFK is that people

always leave with a smile on their face and a feeling of receiving the best service they have ever experienced," Bill says. "We treat each person as Royalty." Thank you, Bill, for reminding us that it is the customer that is the most important. May we never lose sight of this important revelation. You are an unsung hero!

AMY TAYLOR WALDROP is a remarkable young lady from California. Amy has faced overwhelming odds and circumstances that would make an ordinary person give up. Amy was born without a heartbeat, but physicians fought and saved her, a smaller twin born to a drug-addicted mother. She fought for everything in her life from that moment on. At the age of four, she began taking care of her younger brothers and sisters while living in and out of apartments, shelters, or drug-infested motels. Throughout her childhood she suffered violence at the hands of her mom's boyfriends and other adults. By the time she was a teenager, the situation grew worse with her family, as her brothers and sisters were taken away by social workers. After spending six months apart, they were all reunited when they moved in with their grandmother. This lasted for a period of time until, at the age of 18, Amy filed papers to be the legal guardian of her siblings. This was a major uphill battle and proved to be almost more than she could bear. She and her siblings lived in a small, rundown, one-bedroom place that they could barely afford. All of her brothers and sisters were fending for themselves and spending their time getting in trouble.

Instead of enjoying the same things as other teenagers, like homecoming, athletics, and prom, she spent all her time working. She worked as a florist and a waitress. She tried to make enough to survive and keep her family together. But the problems just seemed to get worse and worse with no real hope in sight. She felt like she was alone in the battle.

Amy found some respite from her problems in spending time with a nice young man she had met ... but when she became pregnant, he disappeared. At age 19, Amy gave birth to a child of her own, a little baby boy named Donavin. There she was with a child of her own and still raising her siblings.

If this wasn't challenging enough, she had social workers looking over her shoulder each and every day, trying to ensure every child was getting the best possible care — and it seemed her brothers were no help in convincing the social workers her home was stable.

Finally, she *was* granted permanent custody of her brothers and sisters, and her life began to change. A social worker knew of Royal Family KIDS Camps and told Amy, "You must sign the kids up to go to this camp!" She did so and her brothers Adam, 11, and Joey, 10, attended RFK. She was relieved they would be away for a week. Little did she know this would be the week that changed her brothers' lives.

When she picked Adam and Joey up after a week at camp, the boys were so excited they were talking over each other about what had happened. They raved about their Counselors: Joey talked about Mark, and Adam talked about Fred. They also talked about all the fun activities that they participated in at camp. When the boys got home they pulled out their Memory Bags and began to share with Amy everything they had received at camp. From that day forward, they began to have a new outlook on life and realized that someone really cared for them besides Amy. This began to shape the growing years of their lives. Adam's Counselor, Fred, and his wife, Vicki, still kept in contact with them and helped nurture them through their teenage years.

Amy faced many challenges in her life, but she came out on the other side with victory. Through the help of many supporters, she enrolled at Vanguard University and received a college degree. She received the foster parent award of the year, and she adopted her brothers in 1999. *Reader's Digest* wrote a story about her and her family, and a made-for-TV movie called "Gracie's Choice" was based on their lives. All of her brothers attended RFK, and all were changed by the camp. Amy says, "RFK has given me and the boys spiritual and emotional growth."

Amy now works for a law firm, the same law firm which handled her court case in adopting the boys from the very beginning. Her office represents the majority of the abused, abandoned, and neglected minors in the Orange County Juvenile Dependency System. She loves working with the kids, and truly feels that God put her in that position for a reason. Her past has brought her a lot of insight to her job. Amy has used her experience and has been a glowing example of perseverance and determination. She is a true unsung hero!

Some Christians, although created and designed by God to reach great heights and accomplish great deeds, are satisfied to sit in a pew and wait for others to do the ministry. They have allowed themselves to become stagnant.

Not so with the people involved in Royal Family KIDS Camps. Rather than sitting on the fence posts waiting to hear about God's wonderful healing for abused children, they are actively involved in making a difference in children's lives. They give their prayers, time, talent, and resources; they encourage new staff members or get their own churches involved. Through it all, they are soaring to new heights. They explore and examine the many possibilities for new ministries, and they seize opportunities to participate in great and small ways.

Don't sit on the fence post, watching the opportunities to make a difference pass you by. Join the Unsung Heroes Hall of Fame. Make a difference by following the dream and playing the role that God has appointed for you!

# CHAPTER ELEVEN

# *Reviving a Child's Heart: The New Mission Field*

When we sat down to write this book, the parts about the children — their stories and their words — wrote themselves. But when it came to writing about prevention of child abuse and treatment for offenders, the writing became more difficult. We sense a number of natural barriers.

The obvious one is this: The children we deal with through the camps are generally those whose parents or primary caregivers have been proven so abusive or neglectful that the children have been removed from the home. But hundreds of thousands of children are never removed from abusive environments. And the goal of the foster-care system is — and ought to be — to protect the child.

While it's easy for us to teach children to protect themselves from strangers, we can't protect them from *everybody*; in 75 percent of child maltreatment cases, the perpetrator isn't a stranger. The abuser is a caregiver or a close friend of the family.[1] How can children protect themselves from an abuser who is their parent, caregiver, or guardian?

Children cannot.

Prevention efforts must focus on the abuser, who must be willing to receive help and who probably isn't the kind of person to read a book like this. The problem of how to reach the abuser seems overwhelming.

The other barrier that can thwart the efforts of the Church to respond to the problem of child abuse is that Christians tend to regard hurting a child as the most offensive of crimes. We may find ourselves too angry to pray for the child abuser and too resistant to work toward his or her reclamation. This is a natural, human response. But it *cannot* be the response of the Church on such a critical issue.

We need to accept the example of Jesus, who extended His loving-kindness to the vilest offender, yet at the same time he loved children with all of his perfect nature. A willingness to forgive and help child abusers *does not* erode our compassion for the children. If we can be Christ-like enough to overcome our reluctance to deal charitably with child abusers, we will find the opportunity to help them and to save children from further abuse.

The Christian Church wields an awesome power to heal the scars of child abuse and even to help put back together families that have been broken by it. What is the Church's best response to the secret world of child abuse?

**The New Mission Field**

If your church is like the one we attend, you're helping to support missionaries in a variety of mission fields, not simply foreign missions and home missions as in the past, but numerous special missions as well. These include ministries to handicapped people, to people in the inner city, to substance abusers, to various ethnic groups, to the military, to unwed mothers, to prisoners, and to many others. Each of these ministries is involved in good work for people who desperately need the help.

Let us suggest another important mission field: abused, abandoned, and neglected children. Nearly 3.6 million American children were reported as abused, abandoned, or neglected in

That is a mission field of nearly four million people whom God prizes. God loves children, and He wants us to be His hands and feet and arms to reach abused, abandoned, and neglected children. Jesus said the angels of children always see the face of the Father (Matt. 18:10). The very first way the Christian Church can begin addressing the problems of child abuse in America is to recognize that the abused children are a mission field in need of missionaries. We send missionaries all over the world. Let's send them into the horrific world of abused children.

How do we send them? We can start through support. We can start just like Sean and Mary Evers from California who organized a bike-a-thon in 1995 to help Royal Family KIDS. They called it "From God's Kids to Abused Kids." The bike-a-thon today is known as Tour de O.C. (Orange County) "Gearing Up for Abused Kids" and it is organized by David Brooks. They now feature a 25-mile, a 55-mile, and a 100-mile bike ride all in the Orange County area. Each rider pays a registration fee, plus a support pledge, with the amounts depending on which of three rides they choose. They complete the ride in one day and raise money to help the children. This has been very successful for them and the event draws individuals from all over the state of California. Since starting with nine riders in 1995, this wonderfully organized event has brought out 850 riders (average is 120 riders a year), to raise in excess of over $300,000 for Royal Family KIDS.

The reason this bike-a-thon is so successful is that it reaches beyond the church walls, and reaches the community. Communities will get involved because everyone feels it is ok to raise money for abused, abandoned, and neglected children. They will get behind this purpose because no one wants to see children suffer.

With the combination of creativity, perseverance, and helpful, dedicated volunteers, fundraisers have the potential to become very successful. Often, sponsors help with the cost of the event and donate everything you need to ensure it is successful. Volunteers help make sure nothing is lacking when it comes to following through.

Fundraisers such as this will help bring money into the new mission field without burdening your church or business for the finances. We have found that when causes are presented to businesses and people in the area, they are willing and eager to help.

Another way to help this new mission field is through raising funds to start your own camp or help send kids to one of our already-established camps. Rick Roberts from Norman, Oklahoma, birthed a great idea that can help Directors and churches raise the funds to get involved in this great mission field of abused, abandoned, and neglected children.

After returning from the RFK Leadership Training Conference in March of 2007, and hearing Wes Stafford speak on "it takes a village to raise a child," Rick was spurred by the thought that foster children are not just RFK's and the Church's challenge, but the challenge of the community as well. Sharing this thought with his finance chairman, Rick came up with an idea: He approached the city of Norman and convinced them to proclaim June 20 as "SEND A KID TO CAMP DAY."

The next step was to sell this idea to the local businesses. Since he is a local business owner and sold on the concept himself, it was an easy sell. The idea was to commit a percentage of the day's gross sales to send a kid to camp. He created a list of 100 businesses and was only able to call on approximately 90. Of those 90, he received 100 percent commitment.

Each participating business displayed a 4 x 8 purple banner in front of the store, which read, "SEND A KID TO CAMP PARTICIPANT." In addition, each business displayed a canister for customers to make donations.

By July, they had received about $20,000, which was used to help with the finances of their camp so they could send more kids this past year than ever before. They feel next year the momentum will carry them to even bigger numbers. Even greater than the dollars raised was the awareness in the community of RFK and the chance to support abused, abandoned, and neglected children.

Great ideas such as these can give the dreamer the means to do what is in his or her heart. Don't let the obstacle of "How do I do it?" stop you from moving to action. Children are hanging in the balance. Abuse does not take a vacation, it is an ongoing problem, so we must provide a solution, and giving is the answer.

Don't miss the opportunity to be a part of this new mission field; get on the frontlines and help us win this war on abuse. We need more soldiers to help us by holding up the hands of this ministry through support. People like Daniel, who writes:

*The motive behind giving is, "If there is any good thing that I can do, let me do it now, let me not defer nor neglect it, for I shall not pass this way again." In addition to the axiom just expressed, the very first and important rule of investing that I tell people is that you invest with __PEOPLE__, you do not invest in projects or causes.*

*Wayne and Diane are the people I invest in. Their cause is good, and their motives are just. And I trust them!!! I am investing that portion of the assets I am responsible for with them. I know that whatever we give them will be prudently and judiciously used for the purpose intended. This is why I give to Royal Family KIDS.*

Another man named Ronald states:

*I am a believer in supporting efforts that address issues for kids. RFK brings an extraordinary focus to the abuse of kids. Somehow, we must break this cycle that seems to run rampant today. As a long-time supporter of Wayne and Diane, I know that they will spend dollars wisely, augmented by their tremendous hard work — to focus on the issues. It is an honor to be part of the RFK programs.*

You've heard what the children have said about RFK. You've

heard what Counselors, Directors, donors and friends have said about this wonderful ministry. Now is the time to move to action and support this new mission field. Please help us in this pursuit of reviving the hearts of abused, abandoned, and neglected children all around the world. We know that you will be blessed for it, and the children will be eternally grateful and changed.

For more information about starting camps, fundraisers or donating to this new mission field contact us on the web at www.royalfamilykids.org. Feel free to call us at (714) 438-2494 or you can write us at Royal Family KIDS, 3000 W. MacArthur Blvd., Suite 412, Santa Ana, CA 92704. RFK's email address is office@royalfamilykids.org.

# APPENDIX A:

# *It Takes Time:*
# *An Emmaeus Experience*
## A devotional thought by Diane Tesch

*Note: This devotional is used to close every Director's Training class to implore new Camp Directors to allow God to be sovereign and let the children come to Him on their own time, without coercion from adults at camp.*

If you knew you had only three days to live, what would you do for your closest friends?

How would you carry out the plans for such an occasion?

What preparations would you make?

Three days before Christ's death, He arranged an intimate evening with His closest friends. It wasn't a last minute, spur-of-the-moment-affair; He planned for it and even did some behind the scenes preparation Himself.

Luke 22:8-12 says that He sent Peter and John to set up a Passover dinner. When they asked, "Where?" He said: "As you enter the city, a man carrying a jar of water will meet you. Follow him to the house that he enters and say to the owner of the house, 'The Teacher asks: "Where is the guest room where I may eat the Passover with my disciples?"' He will show you a large upper room, all furnished. Make preparations there."

How do you think it was set?

- Finest cloth for the table
- A goblet formed from the finest metals of the day to hold the best wine they could afford to serve, the sweetest, richest flavor
- A basket of the biggest, deep purple grapes and tender figs, set ready to be plucked as the fruit is passed around
- The freshest, most plump loaf of bread, baked and made ready to serve only the closest friends

The room is swept to every corner and crevice. Every detail is given the scrutiny of a palace butler's eye. This is Royal Treatment! No detail is overlooked!

When the guests arrive and share the evening together, a pivotal moment is forever etched in the mind of the guests: Luke 22:19 says, "And he took bread, gave thanks, and broke it." After they had taken part in dinner, they were still confused at the meaning of all this.

Now let's fast-forward the scene: It's now four days after this memorable moment — the world of Christ's best friends has been turned upside down and inside out! They are reeling from the events of the last 96 hours.

Luke 24:13-17

[13] Now that same day two of them were going to a village called Emmaus, about seven miles from Jerusalem. [14] They were talking with each other about everything that had happened. [15] As they talked and discussed these things with each other, Jesus himself came up and walked along with them; [16] But they were kept from recognizing Him. [17] He asked them, "What are you discussing together as you walk along?"

Luke 24: 28-29

[28] As they approached the village to which they were

going, Jesus acted as if He were going further. [29] But they urged Him strongly, "Stay with us, for it is nearly evening; the day is almost over." So He went in to stay with them.

Let's set the scene: Two of them are walking down the road — scratching their heads, trying to twice guess each other's questions as they walk along the dusty road. They can't understand any of it. A person gradually begins to overtake them on their walk. Now He joins the conversation. They look Him straight in the face, as if He is a totally uninformed stranger to the community and asks: "Are you the only visitor to Jerusalem and do not know the things that have happened in these days?"

They try feebly to explain the day's events and help this individual understand their deep loss. Then they took pity on the uninformed traveler and invited Him to have dinner with them at the close of the day.

Verse 30 of Chapter 24 tells us, "When He was at the table with them, He took bread, gave thanks, broke it and began to give it to them." **Then** their eyes were opened and they recognized Him. Instantly, they linked back to the scene they shared four days before.

**There are some parallels with these incidences and a week at Royal Family KIDS Camp for an abused child.**

1.  At Royal Family, we go to any length necessary to provide the best week possible in the lives of these children. Each staff person has a specific task — he/she becomes a "specialist." Each person can put forth his very best energy and abilities to see that his area is planned exceptionally well — the very best of what's required to create a memory of a lifetime for the campers.

2.  The Director is responsible for the many details that must be anticipated — they will plan in advance and direct other camp staff members to carry out their preparations.

This is what Christ did to prepare a special moment for His friends.

3. This week will be so indelibly marked in the children's bank of "happy memories" from a Christ-like person that someday — 4 days later — 2 weeks later — 6 months later — 10 years later — maybe a lifetime later — when they encounter the next "Christ-like" person in their life, they will suddenly say: *"Aha, this person is just like the Christ-like person who cared for me at Royal Family KIDS Camp. I recognize the close likeness of their love and compassion for me."*

Can we be as patient as Christ was when His closest friends of three years didn't "get it" after all they knew about Christ? Can we be patient and allow the seeds that are planted in these children's lives — children who have never been to a Sunday School class or heard the name of God in a loving way — children who don't have all the theology figured out, yet grow at the pace God has for them? That's all we're asking of our Camp Directors and their staff.

It may be then that they will have their Emmaeus Road Experience and suddenly connect with Christ. Until then, we must leave them in God's hands — like Christ did — and give them time to understand all these things that are so familiar to us.

# APPENDIX B:

# 10 Years of Abuse:
## Statistics and Comparisons
### Child Abuse Rates, 1995-2005

These are the latest statistics that have been compiled on child abuse. These rates have dramatically increased over the last 13 years.[1]

| Report Year: | # of Reported Cases: |
|---|---|
| Fiscal Year 2005 | 3.3 million |
| Fiscal Year 2004 | 3 million |
| Fiscal Year 2003 | 2.9 million |
| Fiscal Year 2002 | 1.8 million |
| Fiscal Year 2001 | 1.8 million |
| Fiscal Year 2000 | 1.7 million |
| Fiscal Year 1999 | 2.9 million |
| Fiscal Year 1998 | 2.8 million |
| Fiscal Year 1997 | 3.0 million |
| Fiscal Year 1996 | 1.0 million |
| Fiscal Year 1995 | 1.0 million |

Further reports compiled show a total of 5,352,000 children were determined by the CPS agencies to be victims of abuse or neglect in the 50 states, District of Columbia, and Puerto Rico.[2]

Reports are dated 2002-2007 which were compiled from 2000-2005 data: (As you can see from the graph above, reports of abuse is a much higher number).

Breakdown By Year:

|  |  |
|---|---|
| 2000 — | 879,000 |
| 2001 — | 903,000 |
| 2002 — | 896,000 |
| 2003 — | 903,000 |
| 2004 — | 872,000 |
| 2005 — | 899,000 |
| TOTAL — | 5,352,000 |

5,352,000 cases of child abuse have been reported since the year 2000. That equates to the Anaheim Angel Stadium being filled almost 119 times, Michigan Football Stadium of 111,000 being filled about 48 times. It is more than the number of people in the states of Wyoming, Montana, South Dakota, North Dakota, Nebraska — all of these central plains states combined! It is time that we reach these children, so that this number does not continue to grow. Help us today reach abused, abandoned, and neglected children. Everyone can make a difference in the life of a child. Start today!

# APPENDIX C:

# *Organizational and Support-Group Resources*

*These organizations may provide you and your church family with additional support as you minister to child-abuse victims.*

American Humane Association — Children's Division, American Association for Protection of Children, 63 Iverness Drive East, Englewood, CO 80112; phone: (303) 792-9900. www.americanhumane.org

Canadian Society for the Prevention of Cruelty to Children, 362 Midland Avenue, Box 700, Midland, ON L4R 4P4 Canada; phone: (705) 526-5647. www.empathicparenting.org

Child Welfare League of America, 2345 Crystal Drive, Suite 250, Arlington, VA 22202; phone: (703) 412-2400. www.cwla.org

Childhelp National Child Abuse Hotline: 1345 N. El Centro, Hollywood, CA 90028; phone: (800) 422-4453 [or (800) 4-A-CHILD]. www.childhelp.org

Christian Alliance for Orphans, 6723 Whittier Ave., Suite 202, Mclean, VA 22101; www.christianalliancefororphans.org

For KIDS Sake, Inc., 917 W. 29th Street, Austin, TX 78705; phone: (512) 476-9490. www.for-kids-sake.com

Kempe Center, 1825 Marion St., Denver, CO 80218; phone:
(303) 864-5300. www.kempecenter.org

National Center for Missing & Exploited Children, 699 Prince St.,
Alexandria, VA 22314; phone: (703) 274-3900.
www.missingkids.com

National Committee for Prevention of Child Abuse and Neglect,
332 S. Michigan Ave., Suite 1200, Chicago, IL 60604-4357;
phone: (312) 663-3520.

Parents United International, Inc., 615 15 Street, Modesto, CA
92354; phone: (209) 572-3446.
http://parents_united.tripod.com

Royal Family KIDS, 3000 W. MacArthur Blvd., Suite 412, Santa
Ana, CA 92704; phone: (714) 438-2494.

Spiritual Dimension in Victim Services, P.O. Box 6736, Denver,
CO 80206; phone: (303) 740-8171.

U.S. Dept. of Health and Human Service — National Center on
Child Abuse & Neglect, 370 L'Enfant Promenade, SW,
Washington, D.C. 20447; phone: (800) 843-5678.

# APPENDIX D:

# *Resources for Churches*

As difficult as it is to think about, child sexual abuse still occurs regularly in today's churches. The main reason why: Churches fail to properly screen and train staff and volunteer workers before putting them into service. Resources are available to assist local churches to implement a prevention plan.

**Title:** *Reducing the Risk Kit* -3rd Edition
**Subtitle:** Keeping Your Ministry Safe from Child Sexual Abuse

### Kit Description:

The Reducing the Risk Kit is designed to help institute a complete prevention program, including: screening, interviewing, training, monitoring, and responding. It is equipped with tools to help keep records on children and youth workers, prevent the wrong people from gaining access to children and youth, and have a fully-trained youth and child protection ministry staff. The complete kit includes a *Training DVD* with ten video training segments, one *Leader's Guide*, ten *Trainee Workbooks*, and ten *Legal Forms & Records Files*. (If desired, each resource can be ordered separately.)

### Individual Item Descriptions:
### Training DVD

This comprehensive *Training DVD* includes 10 stimulating segments with expert teaching from Richard Hammar and a panel of experts, plus personal testimonies, and how-to scenarios. The video training segments include:

1) Child Protection as the Foundation of Your Ministry

2) A Victim's Story

3) Sexual Abuse in Faith Communities — An Expert Roundtable

4) Testimony of a Sex Offender

5) Screening & Selection: Your First Line of Defense (with Richard Hammar)

6) Screening & Selection: The Candidate (a short film)

7) Legal Requirements: The Church's Responsibility to Protect Kids (with Richard Hammar)

8) Supervising Scenarios: What Would You Do?

9) Responding to an Allegation

10) Taking the Next Steps

### Leader's Guide

The *Reducing the Risk Leader's Guide* helps implement the complete *Reducing the Risk Kit*. It also provides additional information on the importance of screening and the reality of child sexual abuse in today's churches.

### Trainee Workbook

Volunteers and staff can rely on their individual *Trainee*

*Workbook* to supplement training session(s). The workbook follows the *Training DVD* video segments plus provides additional key elements not found in the videos. Workers will go home with greater knowledge and a desire to help implement the new child protection strategies. The workbook includes a tear-out test for each trainee to take and turn in to keep in their personal *Legal Forms & Records File.*

### Legal Forms & Records File

Be assured that all important aspects of the screening process are completed and documented using an individual *Legal Forms & Records File* for each person trained. The booklet includes a tear-out application, interview form, reference check forms, and a folder to keep documentation in. To order call 1-800-222-1840 or visit www.YourChurchResources.com.

# ENDNOTES

## Chapter 1

1. "Child Maltreatment 2005." The 16th Annual Publication of the U.S. Department of Health & Human Services Administration for Children and Families Administration on Children, Youth and Families – Children's Bureau, 16.

## Chapter 2

1. Angela Carl, Child Abuse (Cincinnati: Standard, 1985), 24.

2. Jeanne Giovannoni and Rosina M. Becessa, Defining Child Abuse (New York: Free Press, 1979), 14.

3. Carl, Child Abuse, 24.

4. Ray E. Helfer and Henry C. Kempe, The Battered Child Syndrome (Chicago: University of Chicago Press, 1968).

5. "Child Maltreatment 2005," Chapter 4.

6. "Child Maltreatment 2005," 16.

7. Ibid.

8. "Who were the Child Victims?" in "Child Maltreatment 2005," 16-17.

9. "Darkness to Light: Confronting Child Sexual Abuse with Courage." Accessed online 9/8/2007 at http://www. darkness2light.org/KnowAbout/statistics_2.asp.

10. Ibid.

11. "Who is responsible for the abuse and neglect?" in "Child Maltreatment 2005," 17.

12. Dr. Richard Gelles. Family Violence (Beverly Hills, California: Sage Publications, Inc., 1979).

13. Colorado Department of Corrections, 1995.(Cited in the Annual Report of Accomplishments & Results (2001) for Colorado '99-'04 Plan of Work as true in 2001). Accessed online at http://www.reeis.usda.gov/ web/areera/CES.CO.report.2001.pdf.

14. R. Barri Flowers, Runaway Kids and Teenage Prostitution: America's Lost, Abandoned, and Sexually Exploited Children (Praeger Paperback, 2001).

15. "Darkness to Light: Confronting Child Sexual Abuse with Courage." Accessed online 9/8/2007 at http://www. darkness2light.org/KnowAbout/statistics_2.asp.

Chapter 3

1. D. Delaplane and A. Delaplane. Victims of Child Abuse, Domestic Violence, Elder Abuse, Rape, Robbery, Assault, and

Violent Death: A Manual for Clergy and Congregations. Special Edition for Military Chaplains.

2. Maria Roy, Children in the Crossfire (Deerfield Beach, Fla.: Health Communications Inc., 1968), 87-88.

3. James J. Mead and Glenn M. Balch, Jr., Child Abuse and the Church: A New Mission (Costa Mesa, Calif.: HDL Publishing, 1987), 53.

4. Delaplane, Victims of Child Abuse.

Chapter 4

1. "Child Maltreatment 2005," 16.

2. Ken Graber, M.A. Ghosts in the Bedroom: A Guide for Partners of Incest Survivors (Deerfield Beach, FL: Health Communications, Inc., 1991), 1.

3. Jim Hopper, PhD [Harvard Medical School], "Sexual Abuse of Males: Prevalence, Possible Lasting Effects, and Resources." Accessed online at http://www.jimhopper.com/male-ab/. Last Revised 6/7/2007.

Chapter 7

1. Adele Mayer, Sexual Abuse: Causes, Consequences, and Treatment of Incestuous and Pedophilic Acts (Holmes Beach, Calif.: Learning Publications, 1985), 6.

2. Christine Courtois, "Healing the Incest Wound: Adult Survivors in Therapy," WW Norton & Co, New York, 1988.

Accessed online 8/28/2007 from http://www.
advocatesforyouth.org/PUBLICATIONS/factsheet/
fsabuse1.htm#3.

3.  Mayer, Sexual Abuse, 7.

4.  "Motivations for Running Away" (National Runaway
    Switchboard). Accessed 8/28/2007 at http://www.
    1800runaway.org/news_events/third.html. Primary source
    cited as: B. Molnar, S. Shade, A. Kral, R. Booth, R. & J.
    Watters, (1998). "Suicidal Behavior and Sexual / Physical
    Abuse Among Street Youth." Child Abuse & Neglect. Vol. 22,
    NO. 3, 213-222.

5.  "Risk Factors Associated with Running Away" (National
    Runaway Switchboard). Accessed Online 8/28/2007 at
    http://www.1800runaway.org/news_events/third.html.
    Primary source cited as: H. Hammer, D. Finkelhor, & A.
    Sedlak. (2002). "Runaway/Thrownaway Children: National
    Estimates and Characteristics." National Incidence Studies of
    Missing, Abducted, Runaway, and Thrownaway Children
    (Office of Juvenile Justice and Delinquency Prevention).

6.  Dayan Edwards and Eliana Gil, Breaking the Cycle:
    Assessment and Treatment of Child Abuse (Los Angeles:
    Cambridge Graduate School of Psychology, 1986), 91.

7.  National Crime Victimization Survey, 2005. As referenced:
    Rape, Abuse, and Incest National Network (RAINN). 2005
    Statistics. Accessed online 8/28/2007 at http://www.rainn.
    org/statistics/index.html.

8.  "Victims of Sexual Assault: Women/Men Rape, Abuse, and
    Incest National Network (RAINN)." Accessed online

8/28/2007 at http://www.rainn.org/statistics/victims-of-sexual-assault.html. Primary Source: National Crime Victimization Survey, 2003. (Department of Justice). Accessed 8/28/2007 at http://www.rainn.org/docs/statistics/cv03.pdf.

9.   Flora Colao and Tamar Hosansky, Your Child Should Know (New York: Berkley, 1985), 51.

10.  Jacqueline Blais and Carolyn Pesce, "Rape Called Enormous Problem" (USA Today, 23 April 1992), 6A.

11.  "The National Center for Victims of Crime: Incest." Accessed online 9/8/2007 at http://www.ncvc.org/ncvc/main.aspx?dbName=DocumentViewer&DocumentID=32360. Primary Source: Robert Hayes, "Child Sexual Abuse" (Crime Prevention Journal, Summer, 1990).

12.  "The National Center for Victims of Crime: Incest." Accessed online 9/8/2007 at http://www.ncvc.org/ncvc/main.aspx?dbName=DocumentViewer&DocumentID=32360. Primary Source: Patrick Langan and Caroline Harlow (1994). "Child Rape Victims, 1992." Washington, DC: Bureau of Justice Statistics, U.S. Department of Justice.

13.  Mayer, Sexual Abuse, 8.

14.  Lynn Heitritter and Jeanette Vought, Helping Victims of Sexual Abuse (Minneapolis: Bethany, 1989), 91.

15.  Susanne Sgroi, Handbook of Clinical Intervention in Sexual Abuse (Lexington, Mass.: D.C. Heath, 1982), 218.

16.  Edwards and Gil, Breaking the Cycle, 96.

17. Mark Mayfield, "Man Convicted in N.C. Child Sex Abuse Case"(USA Today, 23 April 1992), 6A.

18. Kenneth V. Lanning, "Child Protection Alert" (FBI Law Enforcement Bulletin, January, 1984), 10.

19. A. N. Groth and C. M. Loredo, "Juvenile Sexual Offenders: Guidelines for Assessment" (International Journal of Offender Therapy and Comparative Criminology 25:3): 31-39.

20. Juvenile Justice Bulletin, Nov 1998 OJJDP: U.S. Department of Justice. Accessed online 9/9/2007 at http://www.yellodyno.com/html/child_molester_stats.html.

21. Michael O'Brien and Walter Bera, "Adolescent sexual Offenders: A Descriptive Typology" (Preventing Sexual Abuse 1:3), 1.

22. Heitritter and Bought, Helping Victims of Sexual Abuse, 92.

23. Edwards and Gil, Breaking the Cycle, 92-95.

24. Ibid., 98.

Chapter 8

1. "Child Maltreatment 2005," 16.

Chapter 11

1. "Who is responsible for the abuse and neglect?" in "Child Maltreatment 2005," 17.

2. "Child Maltreatment 2005," 16.

Appendix A

1. Devotional: "It Takes Time: An Emmaeus Experience," by Diane Tesch.

Appendix B

1. Child Maltreatment Reports, U.S. Department of Health and Human Services. Accessed online at http://www. acf.dhhs.gov/programs/cb/stats_research/index.htm.

2. Ibid.

# ANNOTATED BIBLIOGRAPHY

Anderson, B. *When Child Abuse Comes to Church* (Minneapolis: Bethany, 1992). This 174-page paperback is written from a pastor's heart. It includes the chapters "How to Deal with the Media," "Roadblocks to Healing," and "Prevention."

Deleplane, David. *Victims: Manual for Clergy and Congregation* (Washington, D.C.: National Victim Resource Center, 1993). A guide for clergy and religious leaders on responding to the needs of victims of crime.

Gil, Eliana. *Outgrowing the Pain* (New York: Dell, 1983). This 88-page paperback provides a concise overview of victims' feelings, experiences, and reactions in response to abuse in their past. It is recommended to help victims and to help their friends and family better understand some of what those who have been abused feel, think, and act out.

Hammar, Richard, Steven Klipowicz, and James Cobble, Jr. *Reducing the Risk of Child Sexual Abuse in Your Church* (Matthews, N.C.: Christianity Today International, 1993). Complete and practical guidebook for prevention and risk reductions. Includes a major section on policy formation for churches.

Johnson, Becca Cowan and For KIDS Sake, Inc. *For Their Sake: Recognizing and Responding to Child Abuse* (American Camping Association, 1992). This 204-page paperback is designed to assist camp directors and staff, youth ministry leaders, teachers and principals, and child-care providers. She writes the book from her vast knowledge of education and camping.

Mead, James J., Glenn Balch, and Elizabeth Maggio, *Investigating Child Abuse* (Chino, Calif.: R. C. Law & Co., 1992). No longer in print.

Sanford, Doris. *Hurts of Childhood* and *In Our Neighborhood* series. No longer in print.

# CHILD ABUSE RESOURCES

Bender, D. and Leone, B (1994) Child abuse: Opposing Viewpoint. San Diego: Greenhaven Press.

Dubowitz, H. (ed.) (1999) Neglected Children: Research, Practice, and Policy. Thousand Oaks, CA: Sage.

Hadyn. T. (1991) Ghost Girl. New York: Avon Books.

Johnson, B.C. (1992) For Their Sake: Recognizing, Responding to, and Reporting Child Abuse. Martinsville, IN: American Camping Association.

Pelzer, D. (1995) A Child Called It. Deerfield Beach, FL: Health Communications.

Quinn, P.E. (1984) Cry Out! Inside the Terrifying World of an Abused Child. Nashville, TN: Abingdon Press.

Shelman, E.A. (1998) Out of the Darkness: The Story of Mary Ellen Wilson. Lake Forest, CA: Dolphin Moon.

Silverman, S.W. (1996) Because I Remember Terror, Father, I Remember You. Athens, GA: University of Georgia Press.

Tesch, W., Tesch, D. & Benzinger, J. (2000) Moments Matter: The Stories of Royal Family KIDS Camps. Santa Ana, CA: Royal Family KIDS.

VanDam, Carla (2001) Identifying Child Molesters: Preventing Child Sexual Abuse by Recognizing the Patterns of Offenders. New York: Hawthorn Maltreatment and Trauma Press.

# ABOUT THE AUTHORS

**Wayne and Diane Tesch, Founders of Royal Family KIDS**

For 18 years Wayne and Diane Tesch served on the staff of Newport-Mesa Christian Center in Costa Mesa, California, where Wayne was the senior associate pastor. Their ministry brought hundreds of people through their home as new programs and ministries were formed and nurtured. These ministries included dual-career workshops, engaged-couples seminars, adult-leadership training, day camps, resident camps, and in 1985 a camp designed for abused, abandoned, and neglected children.

Wayne's gifts as a visionary, encourager, trainer, and mentor combined with Diane's administrative skills and franchise-training background formed a dynamic husband-wife team to launch and establish Royal Family KIDS, a full-time, nationwide ministry to abused, abandoned, and neglected children — the only one of its kind.

The love and compassion Wayne and Diane Tesch feel for children has always drawn them to meeting the needs of kids in both their church and the community. In 1990, Royal Family KIDS was designed to meet the unique and unusual needs of abused and neglected children, giving them hope and assurance that there are loving adults who care deeply about them. The week-long summer camps have received enthusiastic response and endorsement from the county social-service agencies in 38 states whose subjects have benefited from their camping program.

Currently, Wayne and Diane travel across America and occasionally around the world on behalf of Royal Family KIDS, seeking to mobilize churches that will commit one week each summer to launch a camp for abused, abandoned, and neglected children through the local church community, duplicating the training model first established in Southern California. Their goal is to offer RFK to 100,000 children in the foster system in the US by 2030.

Wayne Tesch has been a member of the Child Abuse Council of Orange County. He has also served on the eight-member advisory board to clergy for the California Consortium for Prevention of Child Abuse, a state-funded agency. Diane has been a two-time nominee by the Red Cross as a Clara Barton Award Recipient in Orange County, California. Together they have authored two other books: Unlocking the Secret World and Moments Matter. Both have been contributing authors to men's and women's devotional books published by Onward Books, Inc., Springfield, Missouri.

The Tesches reside in California and may be contacted at Royal Family KIDS, www.royalfamilykids.org. or (714) 438-2494.

## How Did *You* Survive?

If you were abused as a child, you may have been shaped by a person or program that helped you overcome the scars of your past. Or you may be one of our former campers and we'd love to hear from you. Please share your story in writing with Wayne and Diane Tesch for possible inclusion in a future book. Fill out the coupon below, and include the name, address, and phone number of a pastor, teacher, or adult friend who can verify your story. You may also communicate with us through our email at office@royalfamilykids.org or www.royalfamilykids.org. Thank you, and may God continue to guide you on the road to healing and spiritual health.

YOUR NAME: _____

ADDRESS:_____

CITY:_____STATE:_____ZIP:_____

PHONE: (_____) _____

BIRTHDAY:_____/_____/_____  ☐ Male  ☐ Female

EMAIL:_____

NAME OF REFERENCE: _____

ADDRESS:_____

CITY:_____STATE:_____ZIP:_____

PHONE: (_____) _____

EMAIL:_____

RELATIONSHIP TO YOU:_____

Please type or print your story and the key elements of success in overcoming the long-lasting effects of child abuse, and return the document with this coupon to:

Royal Family KIDS
Attn: Communications Department
3000 W. MacArthur Blvd. Suite 412, Santa Ana, CA 92704
(714) 438-2494
www.royalfamilykids.org / email: office@royalfamilykids.org

I would like a copy of the Royal Family KIDS explanatory video, "Pulling Up Stakes." Please use my donation to continue expanding Royal Family KIDS Camps and helping the abused, abandoned, and neglected children of America find hope and healing. I have enclosed a gift of:

☐ $100  ☐ $50  ☐ $25  ☐ $_____

NAME:_____

ADDRESS: _____

CITY:_____ STATE:_____ ZIP: _____

EMAIL:_____

PHONE: _____

Thank you for your love and generosity. Royal Family KIDS is a nonprofit organization. IRS regulations allow you to deduct the portion of your gift over the cost of the video; you will be sent a receipt for that amount.

Please send your gift today:

Royal Family KIDS
3000 W. MacArthur Blvd. Suite 412
Santa Ana, CA 92704
(714) 438-2494
email: office@royalfamilykids.org